CRANKY'S COOKBOOK

CRANKY'S COOKBOOK

SEAFOOD
&
SHELLFISH
&
SNAILS
&
RAREBITS
&
HUSHPUPPIES
&
EGGS

Walter Hoving

iUniverse, Inc.
New York Bloomington Shanghai

CRANKY'S COOKBOOK
SEAFOOD & SHELLFISH & SNAILS & RAREBITS & HUSHPUPPIES & EGGS

Copyright © 2008 by Walter Hoving

All rights reserved. No part of this book may be used or reproduced by any means, graphic, electronic, or mechanical, including photocopying, recording, taping or by any information storage retrieval system without the written permission of the publisher except in the case of brief quotations embodied in critical articles and reviews.

iUniverse books may be ordered through booksellers or by contacting:

iUniverse
1663 Liberty Drive
Bloomington, IN 47403
www.iuniverse.com
1-800-Authors (1-800-288-4677)

Because of the dynamic nature of the Internet, any Web addresses or links contained in this book may have changed since publication and may no longer be valid.

The views expressed in this work are solely those of the author and do not necessarily reflect the views of the publisher, and the publisher hereby disclaims any responsibility for them.

ISBN: 978-0-595-49486-6 (pbk)
ISBN: 978-0-595-61123-2 (ebk)

Printed in the United States of America

Dedication

To Susan, a woman who has been through 12 years of frustration that have passed since the beginnings of these mental meanderings that have finally come to fruition. She has been my housemate, my companion, my guru and my lover … most of all, my friend. I owe her more than can be counted in my wildest of dreams.

Contents

Foreword ix
Preface xi
Author's Note xiii
Author's Thoughts xv
Appeteasers, Supper Snacks, Theatre Snacks And Party Snacks 1
"To Shuck or not to Shuck, That is the Question" 9
The Early History of Soup-Maybe!!! 38
Fins, Shells and Such 62
Facts You Possibly Didn't Know about Seafood 63
A Buying Guide for Seafood 72
Seafood Handling Guide 75
Cranky's 100 Tips for the Cook 77
Whole Live Maine Lobster 108
Some Personal Lobster Hunting Experience 110
"Shrimps are good and shrimps are fine" 124
Bibliography 183
Restaurants, Cocktail Lounges, Saloons and Parties that Helped to
    Make These Cookbooks Possible 185
Index 203

Foreword

You will quickly realize that I use mostly fresh items, including herbs and spices, that I always try to make my own stocks and always recycle items that later can be used for making sauces and stocks. That is what your freezer is meant to be used for your benefit and the world of Mother Nature.

This cookbook is the first in a series of cookbooks that Cranky intends to publish within the next twelve months. They will be titled:

Cranky's Cookbook & Kitchen Helper-Seafood & Shellfish & Snails & Rarebits & Hushpuppies & Eggs;

Cranky's Cookbook & Kitchen Helper-Appetizers & Soups & Stews & Potées & Pies & Bourrides & Cassoulets & Ragouts;

Cranky's Cookbook & Kitchen Helper-Bouillabaisse-A Tale of One City or The Creations of Hungry Fishermen;

All of these books are collections of information, folklore and recipes from the world over. Some of these tried and proven winners find their beginnings prior to the Middle Ages, while others have been created by all of the great chefs, chefs such as the Great Careme, and including the humble housewife and house-husband in every home in the world. It is the intention of this writer to change what some homemakers consider drudgery into a pleasant and rewarding experience. I believe that this cookbook will assist in the understanding pf the simple procedures in food preparation that, at first might seem complicated and bordering on tedium, and will turn cooking into a pleasurable experience. Most cooks get settled into a repetitive direction because of limitation of time caused by profession, job restrictions, family obligations and hundreds of life's distractions. This causes many of us to plan, prepare and serve the same boring, humdrum meals to our loved ones or guests, day after week after month after year.

One way to get of a culinary rut is to plan ahead. When you make BBQ Sauce, a salad dressing, spaghetti sauce, a marinade or any stock or broth … triple the recipe … quadruple the recipe … then cool and store in mason jars or perhaps in saved mayonnaise jars that you bring home weekly from the supermarket. These can be sealed tightly and stored in the refrigerator for a very long time. If you intend to freeze them … freeze them without the lids because of expansion … seal tightly and they will last for months. This will make the preparation of future meals more relaxing and turn cooking into fun and your life will be less stressful. I have included some of these recipes in this cookbook that will help you to join the millions of peoples throughout the world that frolic daily through the culinary world, experiencing the inexhaustible plethora of recipes from the vast world of gustatory delights.

Thank you for purchasing this cookbook and I am sure that it will become an important part of your cookbook collection as well as your culinary creativity.

Preface

"In order to see the world in a better light, with clear vision and an alert mind, one must have good health, a full stomach, the appropriate wine, and the time to enjoy … hence, if you invite a guest to dinner … you take charge of their happiness while under your roof."

A man, whose name I never knew, made that statement after his third double martini at the old Wrigley Building Men's Bar that is now part of the past.

I have tried to make this a cookbook that consisted of fine and unusual recipes from the entire world … complete with their very unique names and idiosyncrasies. I have attempted to add an appropriate amount of humor, to make the drudgery of the kitchen turn into an adventure of creation and of love.

In addition, there are some very interesting paragraphs sprinkled through the text that add a good deal of humorous and silly information as to the backgrounds and origins of some of the dishes … in order to improve your Trivial Pursuit scores.

Hopefully, after you peruse this volume of food mirth, you will begin to understand the courage of those original tasters of the first slug or snail, swallowed the first live oyster or razor clam … live and wiggly, or steamed an ugly Maine lobster in its own water and seaweed.

Such delicacies as Toad-in-the-Hole, Raggedy Soup, Soused Mackerel, Potted Shrimp, Bubble and Squeak, Welsh Rabbit, Pockets of Brains, Trout à la Jesus, Impossible Pie, Trifle and Hoppel Poppel can be found in the index of this cookbook but I assure you that you will have more fun finding them as you explore the pure nonsense of these pages.

I will leave you with this toast to life.

"May your every gustatory delight be realized and may we all enjoy fine food and fine drink, and good health, and much wealth, your share of love, and, the time to spend them all."

Author's Note

It has long been established by the adventurers of mankind, the explorers of the unknown and the courageous desires of the chosen few that the world was and is full of unknown delights. It is these explorers of the unknown to whom we should be thankful for these those tasty treats that arrive on our table from the supermarket just around the corner. We should all take a moment of silence for all of those who, through great curiosity and maximum effort, supply the markets with these fruits of their labor.

From every culture, down through the centuries of time, mankind has accumulated a vast amount of knowledge and information that has kept our palates satisfied, our energies renewed, and taught us to utilize the curious and wonderful resources of "Mother Nature's Kitchen."

Truly, I wish to thank those who have traversed the globe from east to west, then, then south; tasting of the new and the different and the strange. To these travelers, chefs and adventurers, we owe thanks for the hundreds of recipes that we should never take for granted ... some of which ... appear in this cookbook.

Bon Appetit

Author's Thoughts

Mankind's ancestors, before he taught himself to stand on his hind legs, would forage and prey on other game or plant life until he had gorged himself, nearly always retiring to his lair to sleep.

This changed radically when mankind stated to live in groups or tribes or social settlements … hence the creation of what we now call the meal, which gave rise to the feast, the celebration of the Gods, the memory or anniversary of an event of importance such as a wedding, a win, a wake, a holiday and even the lowly birthday. Most of the early feasts or celebrations were based on religious beliefs and to this day are celebrated in area and countries of the world long separated from idol worship and Paganism.

Man is a social animal and will celebrate just about anything from a birthday, a marriage, a death, a victory, a holy day, an election, the spring planting, the autumn harvesting, He will have a festival to the fertility Gods for a healthy child, many children or a good crop. He has always prepared giant boards of food for just about any event. We all love a party!

While in grade school, a teacher mentioned that the first recorded celebration of a person's death, at least in book form, could be found in Homer's Iliad. After Hector's death at the hands of Achilles, King Priam ends the day of his son's death with a feast … the first recorded wake in mankind's long history.

It is probably agreed by most archaeologists and anthropologists that the existence of fire in Mankind's history dates back about750,000 years to place in France in the Durance Valley, but it wasn't until about 12,000 years ago that man went from roasting his catch over an open flame to use of a spit over coals, to the use of water for boiling and then the covering of the fire with a stone slab to keep the rain out, thus creating the first grill for frying and the very first oven or kiln for baking.

Ah! Yes, the pleasures of the barbeque. I truly believe that the barbeque satisfies a definitive primordial instinct in modern man. "Oh, yes, we have come a long way, baby."

"Really!"

Appeteasers, Supper Snacks, Theatre Snacks And Party Snacks

Most recipes in this cookbook can be adapted to be served as an appetizer or an entree.

No matter the preparation, the size of the portion, basically, is what determines one section of a cookbook from another. The main goal of an appetizer is to tweek a person's appetite and not to destroy it. As to a late snack or theatre snack, most of the time with a nightcap … it shouldn't give you heartburn.

A good recipe should make one's appetite more curious and hungry for satisfaction. Appetizers should never be filling … they should only serve as catalysts to the taste buds and imaginations that await the future wonders of your cuisine.

Cranky's Beer Shrimp

This combination of ingredients doesn't sound logical, but it turns out to be a delightful taste treat.

48 raw shrimp in the shell (21-25 count)
2 16 oz. cans of beer
4 cups Cranky's Meat Sauce
4 Cloves garlic (minced)
8 slices of bread
6 tbsp garlic butter

Poach the shrimp in salt water until slightly curled and reddish in color. Peel and devein the shrimp and set aside. Pour the beer, meat sauce and the garlic in a saucepan and reduce until desired thickness. Lightly sauté the bread in the garlic butter until golden brown in a skillet, trim the edges and cut diagonally. Place six shrimp in each au gratin dish and smother with the sauce. Grind up the bread trims up and sprinkle on the top and bake in a hot oven until the sauce starts to bubble. Place two halves of the toasted bread in the sauce. (Serves 8)

Cranky's Shrimp Sautéed in Garlic

48 raw shrimp in the shell (21-25 count)
5-6 garlic cloves (minced)
¼ cup brandy or Cognac
½ tsp. Cranky's Fines Herbes
½ tsp. Cranky's Seafood Seasoning Salt
2 lemons (wedged)

Split the shrimp down the back and remove the veins, leaving the shells and the tails intact. Melt the butter in a large sauté pan and add the minced garlic and the shrimp. Toss the shrimp gently a couple of times. Add the fines herbs and the seasoning salt. Simmer the mixture, tossing frequently until all of the shrimps are curled and reddish pink in color. This should take about 3-4 minutes. Do not over-cook. Flame the mixture with the brandy or the Cognac. Serve in small bowls with the lemon wedges and pan juices. (Serves 8)

Cranky's Potted Shrimp

I found this little tidbit in the Bahamas, but I was told that it originated in England at Harrods.

1-2 pounds of butter
1 tsp. mace (ground)
½ tsp. nutmeg (freshly ground)
1 tsp. sea salt
1 pound of raw shrimp (21-25 count, peeled and deveined)
Melba toast or Swedish hard bread

If you are going to serve this on Friday, this should be prepared in a large mold on Wednesday or Thursday, and stored in the refrigerator so that all of the tastes become engaged. Sauté the shrimp in melted butter but do not over cook the shrimp. Simmer the shrimp until slightly curled and light pink. Add the mace, nutmeg and sea salt. Make sure that all of the shrimp are covered by the mixture. Refrigerate the bowl and serve on Friday with the Melba Toast or Swedish hard bread. I normally make the canapés so that all of the guests get some. (Serves 8)

Cranky's Shrimp Toast

1 pound shrimp (peeled and deveined)
7-8 water chestnuts
1 ½ tsp. sugar
1 tsp. sea salt
2 tbsp. dill (freshly chopped)
2 eggs (lightly beaten)
2 tbsp. corn starch
3-4 cups peanut oil

In a large glass bowl mince the ray shrimp along with the dill, water chestnuts, sea salt, sugar, cornstarch and lightly beaten eggs. You can also do this in a food processor or a blender. Trim the crusts off the bread and cut each piece into 4 triangles. Spread each triangle with one tsp. of the shrimp mixture. Heat the peanut oil to 400-450 degrees. Lower the shrimp triangles into the oil, a few at a time with a slotted spoon with the shrimp side down. Turn over after 45 seconds and fry until golden brown. Remove to a piece of brown paper to drain. (Makes 48 taste treats)

Cranky's Shrimp and Artichokes in Peppery Butter Sauce

8 artichokes (medium size)
4 cloves garlic (minced)
4 tbsp. lemon juice (freshly squeezed)
4 tbsp. black pepper (freshly ground)
¼ cup Worcestershire sauce
2 tsp. Tabasco sauce
2 tsp. basil (freshly chopped)
1 tsp. sea salt
2 tsp. oregano (freshly chopped)
½ tsp. cayenne
1 pound butter
32 medium shrimp in their shells
1 cup scallions (minced)

Cut off the bottom stems of the artichokes and even out so that they stand up on their own. With a serrated knife trim about one inch off the entire top of the artichoke. Boil the artichokes in salted water until the bottom flesh is tender to a knife poke. Drop the garlic into a food processor and mince along with the lemon juice, black pepper, Worcestershire sauce, Tabasco sauce, basil, salt, oregano and the cayenne pepper and blend well. Add the butter and blend some more. Mix the scallions and this mixture with the shrimp and bake until the shrimp curl up, but not tightly. Invert the artichokes so that they drain. Remove the center leaves of the artichokes and fill the cavity of all eight with the cooked shrimp mixture. (Serves 8)

Cranky's Caviar

I love caviar! The only problem is that the good caviar costs a great deal. Good quality caviar such as Osietr, Sevruga and Sterlet are extremely expensive but worth every dollar spent. Sterlet caviar is virtually unobtainable because of the rarity of the fish and none is exported from Russia. This is the "legendary gold" caviar of the Czars and I personally have never tasted it. However, since we are relegated to these other "inferior products," we will just have to rough it out with Beluga or Osietr.

8 ounces fresh Beluga Caviar
1 large basket of thin toast
2 qts. Russian vodka (chilled in the freezer or in a block of ice)
1 cup hard boiled egg yolks (finely chopped)
1 cup hard boiled egg whites (finely chopped)
2 tbsp. parsley (freshly chopped)
½ cup green onions (freshly chopped)
1-2 sour cream
8 pony glasses (chilled in the freezer)

Place the sour cream, egg yolks, egg whites, parsley and onions in individual glass bowls on a lazy Susan with the caviar in a glass bowl in the middle. Use only stainless steel utensils. Seafood and silver do not mix. The caviar should be left in the original container so that the eggs do not get bruised. Bury the container in a glass bowl filled with crushed ice. Do not forget the basket of toast. My guests normally put a dollop of sour cream on the toast followed by pinches of the other items and topped with the caviar. This creation is quite tasty when popped in the mouth and followed by a pony glass three quarters full of ice cold vodka. Most people like this. However, I prefer to just use very little sour cream, just enough to keep the caviar on the toast and then popped into the mouth. Then you will get the full salty vanilla nutlike flavor of the caviar … then follow it with the ice cold vodka to "wash it down" so to speak. (Serves 8)

Cranky's Caviar Supreme

1 cup caviar
1 tbsp. onion (grated)
1 tsp. lemon juice
3 tsp. vegetable oil
16 slices of toast (trimmed and diagonally cut)
4 tbsp. butter
2 tsp. parsley (freshly chopped)
Lemon wedges

Gentle rinse the caviar in a fine strainer and place it in a glass bowl. Add the onion, lemon juice and oil and gently toss with a rubber spatula. Cover and marinate in the refrigerator overnight. Butter the toast triangles, spread with the caviar mixture and bake them on a cookie sheet in a 450 degree oven for 2 minutes. Garnish with the parsley and the lemon wedges. (Serves 8)

Cranky's Salmon Eggs Columbia River

2 dozen hard boiled eggs
1 cup freshly poached salmon
2 tsp. onion (finely chopped)
2 pimentos (finely chopped)
½ cup mayonnaise
2 tbsp. lemon juice
1 tsp. sea salt
½ tsp black pepper (freshly ground)
½ tsp cayenne pepper (freshly ground)
2 tbsp parsley (freshly chopped)
1 tsp. cream sherry)
Lemon wedges

Peel the eggs and cut them in half. Place the egg yolks, salmon, onion, pimento, mayonnaise, lemon juice, sea salt, black pepper, cayenne pepper and the sherry in a food processor and blend thoroughly. Fill the egg whites with the salmon mixture, sprinkle with the chopped parsley and serve with the lemon wedges. (Serves 8)

Cranky's Smoked Trout Paté

2 fillets smoked trout (skinned and boned)
6 ounces cream cheese (softened)
3 ozs. soft mild goat cheese
¾ cup unsalted butter (softened
1 scallion (finely chopped)
1 tsp. drained bottled horseradish
2 tbsp. lemon juice
½ tsp. Tabasco sauce
1 tbsp capers (drained)

2 tbsp. parsley freshly chopped)
2 tbsp. chives (freshly chopped)

Blend the trout with the cheeses in a food processor, along with the softened butter. Add the rest of the ingredients and process until very smooth. Transfer the mixture to a crock and chill for two hours. Serve with crackers of your choice. (Serves 8)

Cranky's Smoked Salmon-Stuffed Cherry Tomatoes

1 pt. cherry tomatoes
1 8 oz. package cream cheese (softened)
¼ pound smoked salmon (sliced thin)
4 tsp. dill (freshly minced)
1 tsp lemon juice

Cut each cherry tomato crosswise in half and remove the pulp and the seeds. Place the cherry tomato cups cut size down so they will drain. In a food processor, blend the cream cheese, smoked salmon, dill and lemon juice until the mixture is smooth. Spoon the mixture into a small decorating bag with a star tip and squeeze the mixture into the tomato cups. Arrange the cups on a chilled platter and cover. Refrigerate until ready to serve. (Makes about 48-50 servings)

Cranky's Salmon Mousse a la Beanie

2 packages Knox gelatin
½ cup water
1 cup Cranky's Chicken Stock
4 tbsp dill (freshly chopped)
1 cup Classic Mayonnaise
2 tbsp lemon juice (freshly squeezed)
¼ cup green onions (finely minced)
1 tsp. sea salt
½ tsp. paprika
4 cups poached salmon (poached in milk)
2 cups heavy cream

Combine the water, gelatin, chicken stock and dill in a saucepan and stir over low heat until the gelatin has completely dissolved. Allow to cool. Whisk in the mayonnaise, lemon juice, green onions, sea salt and paprika. Set aside. Poach the salmon, drain and place the salmon meat in the food processor. Process the salmon until very fine. Whisk both mixtures together. Whip the heavy cream until it forms high peaks. Fold this into the salmon and gelatin mixture and pour into a 3 quart mold. Chill for 3-4 hours. When hardened, remove from the mold onto a chilled glass platter. (Serves about 16)

"To Shuck or not to Shuck, That is the Question"

Over the years a great many folk have asked me for the history of the word "shucking," a commonly used term referring to the opening of oysters. After many dead ends in various dictionaries, I will attempt, in the next few paragraphs, to formulate a theory that I believe to be slightly better than theory. In a biography of the great Indian Chief Tecumseh, there is a mention of black and white wampum, the trading vehicle of the times. These strings or strands were made up of sea shells such as oyster, clam and mussel—the value of which depended on the color—the black being worth much more than the white strands. This is thought to be of Algonquian origin. However, the Narragansett Indian, a New England Indian tribe, had a word, "anawsuck," meaning white sea shell, and "suckanhock," meaning black sea shell, and I truly believe that the term shucking has its roots firmly implanted in this early culture. However, I truly believe a much more interesting and diverse origin hides in the wings, so to speak. In Webster's International Dictionary, a shuck is defined as "a shell, a husk, a pod, the outer coverings of a seed or nut, the husk of Indian corn, the shell of an oyster or a clam, something of little or no value." This illustrates an interesting side of the puzzle. In colloquial terms, the slang phrases "to not care shucks"—"shucks"—"not worth shucks"—what you receive for good money from a "huckster"—a "shuckster"—"a con man." In other words, shucks, with exception of wampum, was considered useless merchandise and created by the shucker of corn, the shucker of peas, the shucker of oysters—getting nothing for something from a shuckster—what is left when an oyster is opened and consumed—a shuck. When the women that settled this country prepared for a feast or faire, they would gather together and have a shucking—the preparation of the feast. What was left on the ground were the shucks by the shuckers—hence the derivation of the term.

Cranky's Oysters

Oysters are delicate little creatures with a subtle flavor all their own and must be treated and cooked accordingly ... with gentility and love. The shucking of an oyster as an art and one must not bruise the creatures. When shucking, the large center muscle must be cut from both shells so that the diner doesn't tear the oyster apart trying to remove it from its shell.

50-60 oysters in the shell (the larger the better)
2 cups lump crabmeat (fresh, if possible)
8 strips of bacon (minced)
3-4 cloves garlic (minced)
1 ½ cups bread crumbs
6-8 tbsp. olive oil
2 cups Béchamel sauce
1 cup heavy cream
1 ½ cups Madeira
rock salt
lemon wedges

Shuck the oysters and set aside. Heat the oven to 375 degrees. Mince the bacon and fry on low heat along with half of the garlic until the bacon is crisp. Drain the fat out of the pan and add the crabmeat. Set aside. In another pan, combine the Béchamel sauce, cream and the Madeira. Bring to a quick boil, stirring constantly while adding the crabmeat mixture. Cook for 2 minutes if the crabmeat is fresh ... if not ... turn the heat off immediately. Mix the rest of the garlic, the bread crumbs and the olive oil together and set aside. Place the shucked oysters on a baking sheet that contains a layer of rock salt. Put some of the crab mixture on each oyster and sprinkle each with the breadcrumb mixture. Bake the oysters in the oven for about 4-5 minutes or until the topping is golden brown. Serve at once with lemon wedges. (Serves 8)

Cranky's Oysters Bienville

48 oysters (freshly shucked on the half shell)
3 cups Béchamel Sauce
1 cup white wine
¼ cup Cognac

¼ cup olive oil
¼ cup cooked shrimp (finely chopped)
½ cup green onions (freshly chopped)
½ cup mushrooms (freshly and finely chopped)
1-2 cloves garlic (minced)
1 tbsp Cranky's Hot Like Hell Mustard
¼ tsp. sea salt
½ tsp white pepper (fresh ground)

Shuck the oysters and save the liquor. Place the oysters back in the bottom shells and strain the liquor and save for later. Sauté the onions, the mushrooms and the garlic in the olive oil and when the onions are translucent, add the Béchamel Sauce, the oyster liquor, white wine, the Cognac, Cranky's Hot Like Hell Mustard, sea salt and the white pepper. Simmer until thick and creamy. Place the oysters on a baking sheet and spoon the sauce over the oysters. Bake for 3-4 minutes in a 450 degree oven. Serve at once. (Serves 8)

Cranky's Oysters Lucullus

2 shallots (peeled and finely chopped)
6 tomatoes (peeled, seeded and chopped)
1 tsp. sea salt
1 tsp. paprika
½ cup olive oil
4 ozs. chili sauce
1 tsp. Worcestershire sauce
1-2 ozs. Beluga caviar
40-50 oysters (unshucked)
2 cups white wine fish aspic
3-4 lemons (wedged)
2 tsp. lemon juice
1 tsp. celery salt

Sauté the shallots in a sauce pan. When the shallots are translucent, adding the tomatoes, sea salt, paprika, Worcestershire sauce and the chili sauce. Simmer until the liquid is reduced slightly. Melt the aspic in the microwave and put into a glass bowl. Shuck the oysters over the bowl so that the oyster liquor is saved. Do this through a fine strainer to keep the oyster shell chips out of the liquid. Put the empty shells into some cold water to soak. Refrigerate the oysters in another glass bowl. Add the lemon juice and the celery salt to the aspic mixture and mix well. Place the deeper shells on a large tray and put a teaspoon of the sauce on top of the oyster. Spoon a small dollop of the caviar on each oyster. Cover the oyster with a spoonful of the white wine aspic mixture and refrigerate until firm. Get ready for a taste treat. (Serves 8)

Cranky's Oysters Rockefeller

4-5 dz. large oysters
2 ½-3 cups spinach (fresh chopped)
1 ½ cups parsley (freshly chopped)
1 ½ cups green onions (chopped)
10-12 shallots (chopped)
5-6 tbsp. fennel leaves (chopped)
1 pound butter
2 tbsp. anchovy paste
Tabasco sauce
2 cups bread crumbs
1 cup Ricard or Pernod
1 tsp. sea salt
1 tsp black pepper (freshly ground)
Rock salt

Shuck the oysters over a glass bowl and strain the liquor. Wash the deep halves of the shells and place on a bed of rock salt on a cookie sheet. Blend the parsley, spinach, green onions, fennel and shallots until the mixture is puréed. Melt the butter in a sauce pan and cook this mixture for 4-5minutes on simmer. Stir in a few dashes of hot sauce and the anchovy paste and the bread crumbs. Cook this mixture until smooth. Add the oyster liquor, Ricard and season with the salt and pepper. Put the oysters in the shells and spread the mixture of top of the oysters. Bake in a 400 degree oven for about 5-6 minutes. (Serves 8)

Cranky's Oysters à la Catalina

¼ tbsp Edam cheese (grated)
4 tbsp butter (melted)

2 cups catsup
2 tsp. Worcestershire sauce
1 cup heavy cream
1 ½ cup crabmeat
3-4 tbsp cream sherry
4 dz. oysters (freshly shucked)
Sea salt to taste
Black pepper to taste (freshly ground
8 slices of toast

Heat the cheese and butter in a double boiler until smooth and creamy. Add the Worcestershire sauce and the catsup. Add the cream, crabmeat and the cream sherry and stir constantly. Add the oysters and when the oysters begin to curl, remove from the heat. Season to taste with the sea salt and the pepper and serve on the toast slices in newburg dishes. (Serves 8)

Cranky's Poached and Spiced Oysters

48 Oysters (freshly shucked)
2 cups milk
2 cups white wine
1 tsp. parsley (freshly chopped)
1 tsp. basil (freshly chopped)
1 tsp. allspice (freshly ground)
1 tsp. thyme (freshly chopped)
½ tsp. sea salt
½ tsp. black pepper (freshly ground)
Arrowroot as needed

Shuck the oysters and save the liquor and the bottom shells. Mix the parsley, basil, allspice, thyme, sea salt and the black pepper together in a mortar and pestle, adding a small amount of the white wine. Put the mixture in a glass bowl. Add the rest of the wine and the milk and the oyster liquor. Stir the mixture well, add the oysters, cover and marinate the oysters in the refrigerator for 3-4 hours. Strain the liquor and set the oysters aside. Bring the liquor to a slow simmer, and introduce the oysters, to the simmering liquid with a slotted spoon for 1 minute each. Place the poached oysters in the shells. Thicken the liquid by reduction and the use of the arrowroot, if necessary and ladle the thickened liquid over the oysters. (Serves 8)

Cranky's Oyster Panache

8 Cranky's Oysters a la Catalina
8 Cranky's Oysters Rockefeller
8 Cranky's Oysters Lucullus
8 Cranky's Oysters in Champagne
8 Cranky's Oysters
8 Cranky's Poached and Spiced Oysters
2 lemons (wedged)
Large basket of garlic bread
Rock salt

Prepare all of the oysters as the individual recipes state that are in this section of this cookbook. Place them on heat resistant plates on beds of rock salt and bake until bubbling hot. Serve with the garlic bread. (Serves 8)

Cranky's Oysters in Champagne

4-5 dz. large oysters in the shell
¼ cup shallots (minced)
1 cup Champagne
1 ½ cups Cranky's Hollandaise Sauce
½ cup cream

Shuck the oysters, saving the oyster liquor. Poach the oysters in their own liquor, adding the minced shallots. When the oysters are poached and the shallots are translucent, spoon the oysters back into their shells. Add the Champagne to the liquor in the pan and reduce slightly. Blend this mixture with the hollandaise sauce that has been freshened with the cream. Spoon the finished sauce over the oysters and brown slightly under the broiler. (Serves 8)

Cranky's Baked Scalloped Oysters

3 pts oysters (freshly shucked)
Liquor from the oysters
1 pound butter (melted)

2 cups bread crumbs
1 tsp. white pepper (freshly ground)
1 cup half and half
1 tsp sea salt
½ tsp Worcestershire sauce
Tabasco sauce
1 8 inch cake pans

Drain the oysters, saving the liquor in a glass bowl. Mix the bread crumbs and the softened butter by tossing lightly together. Spread about one third of the mixture on the bottom of the pan and cover with a layer of oysters. Sprinkle with a little sea salt and white pepper. Repeat with another layer of bread crumbs and the rest of the oysters. Season the mixture one more time. Pour the half and half in to the oyster liquor with the Worcestershire sauce and the Tabasco sauce. Mix well and pour the mixture over the oysters and top with the remaining bread crumb mixture. Bake into a 325 degree oven for about 30-35 minutes and serve piping hot. (Serve 8)

Cranky's Angels on Horseback

4 dz. oysters (shucked and drained)
24 strips of bacon (halved and half cooked)
8 skewers
½ cup bread crumbs
¼ cup butter
1 tsp. nutmeg (freshly ground)
2 tsp. parsley (freshly chopped)
Sea salt to taste
Black pepper to taste (freshly ground)
1-2 tsp. paprika
8 pieces of toast (trimmed and lightly buttered)
8-16 lemon wedges

Wrap each oyster in a half cooked bacon strip and place on the skewers. (6 per skewer) Broil briefly under a hot flame. Mix the bread crumbs with butter, nutmeg and chopped parsley and simmer for one minute. When the oysters are cooked, place the skewers on the buttered toast. Cover the oysters with the bread crumb mixture. Sprinkle the dish with paprika and serve piping hot with lemon wedges. (Serve 8)

Cranky's Moules Normande

40-50 fresh mussels
½ cup white wine
1 tbsp. parsley (freshly minced)
1 tbsp. shallots (freshly minced)
1 celery top (freshly and finely chopped)
1-2 tbsp. sweet butter
1 tsp. sea salt
¼ tsp black pepper (freshly ground)
½ cup heavy cream
1 tbsp. butter (regular)
½ tbsp. chervil (freshly chopped)
1 tbsp. parsley (freshly chopped)
1 loaf French bread
¼ cup Calvados Apple Brandy

Scrub the mussels in cold water, removing the barnacles and the little beards. Place the mussels in a pot along the white wine, parsley, shallots, celery, sweet butter, sea salt and the black pepper. Cover the pot and cook until the mussels have all opened. Remove the mussels from the pot and tear off the top shells and discard and keep them warm. Continue to reduce the mussel stock until it has been reduced to one-half. Thicken the cream in a small sauce pan until it is syrupy. Swirl the thickened cream into the mussel stock. Add the regular butter, chervil and one-half of the chopped parsley. Whisk in the Calvados Apple Brandy, place the mussels in soup dishes and pour the sauce liberally over their tops. Brown them lightly in your broiler. Sprinkle with the remaining parsley and serve with the French bread. Serve with a soup spoon, a cocktail fork and the wine of your choice. (Serves 8)

Cranky's Oysters Normande

Prepare in the same manner as Moules Normande, just poach the oysters as opposed to steaming them ... steaming makes oysters tough and chewy.

Cranky's Clams Normande

Prepare in the same manner as Moules Normande, however use small steamer clams, cherrystones are a bit chewy.

Cranky's Lobster Cocktail

16 ozs. Lobster meat (freshly cooked)
2-3 heads Boston lettuce
4 avocados
2 lemons (wedged)
8 ozs. Cranky's Majestic Cocktail Sauce

Cut the lobster meat in bite-size pieces and chill well. Clean and crisp the lettuce leaves. Cut each avocado in half, pit, peel and place half … pit hole up on a bed of lettuce on a chilled plate. Fill the center with 2 ounces of the lobster meat and smother with 1 ounce of Cranky's Majestic Cocktail Sauce. Serve with lemon wedges. (Serves 8)

Cranky's Shrimp Cocktail

32 jumbo shrimp (cooked, peeled and deveined)

The only difference from lobster cocktail is that you put the large ends of the shrimp in the pit hole of the avocado. (Serves 8)

Cranky's Crab Cocktail

16 ozs. jumbo lump crabmeat (canned or fresh but cooked)
8 pineapple rings (freshly sliced)

Follow the instructions for lobster cocktail substituting the pineapple rings for the avocados. (Serves 8)

Cranky's Soused and Stuffed Clams

48 cherrystones
½ cup water
8 slices of toast

2 tbsp. shallots (finely chopped)
1 clove garlic (minced)
4-5 tbsp. butter
1 tbsp. Cognac
1 tbsp. white wine
1 tsp. Pernod
3 tbsp. chives (freshly snipped)
2 cups Cranky's White Wine Fish Aspic
2 lemons (wedged)

Gel the White Wine Fish Aspic on a cookie sheet so that you can cut it into squares at a later time. Scrub the cherrystones and place them in a large steamer pot with the water and steam them until the clams have all opened. Remove from the heat. Place all of the clam meat in a food processor along with ½ cup of clam broth. Save half of the clam shells. Add the Cognac, white wine, the Pernod and the toast and process. Sauté the shallots and the garlic in the butter and add the mixture to the processor. Add the chives at the last minute. Spread the mixture into the clam shells. Chill them well. Chop the White Wine Fish Aspic into small squares and place a square on each clam and serve with lemon wedges and cocktail forks. (Serves 8)

"An Ode to a Clam"

"A mollusc's life is but a sham,
Oh yes, tis' hard to be a clam.
We're misunderstood when purchased live,
Frustrating all shuckers far and wide.

Some folks will steam us silly,
Making our tender bodies extremely chewy.
Others choose to eat us raw,
Discarding our tenderness for size and awe.

Who are these fools that vent their rage,
And bitch, and moan and lose their control.

Ladies and gents be very patient, be very kind
Remember you folks, we have no mind!"

Cranky's Charcoal Roasted Cherrystones

100-120 cherrystones
2 cups butter (melted)
1 lemon (juiced)
1 tsp. sea salt
1 tsp. black pepper (freshly ground)
3-4 tbsp. parsley (freshly chopped)

Shuck the clams and discard the shells. Save and strain the clam juice. Mix the clam juice, the butter, the lemon juice, the salt, the black pepper and the parsley together in a saucepan and simmer the mixture for one minute. Place the clams on a cookie sheet and pour the mixture over them. Cover the pan with aluminum foil and punch a few holes in it … about a dozen or so. Place the sheet on the charcoal grill and close the lid. Allow the clams to roast for about 10-12 minutes. Remove the aluminum foil and let your guests enjoy a truly amazing BBQ treat. (Serves 8-12 People)

Cranky's Steamed Clams

8-10 pounds steamer clams
1 tsp. sea salt
1 tsp black pepper (freshly ground)
2 cups melted butter
2-4 lemons (wedged)

Soak the steamers in cold water for about one hour. Wash them thoroughly; testing each one to insure that there is movement. Discarded all of the ones that do not have any movement because they are probably dead and you never know when a dead clam died. Steam the clams until all are open and serve in large bowls. Strain the broth and serve in mugs with a lemon wedge and melted butter on the side. (Serves 8)

Cranky's Steamed Mussels

48 live mussels (scrubbed and bearded)
1 cup Parmesan cheese (freshly grated)
½ cup parsley (freshly chopped)
1 cup olive oil
1 loaves French bread

Follow the same recipe with the exception of the following. Remove the little beards rather than flicking the non-existent necks and serve with French bread dipped in olive oil and sprinkled with Parmesan cheese and fresh parsley. A nicely chilled bottle augments this tasty treat. (Serves 8)

Cranky's Stuffed Mussels

4 pounds mussels (scrubbed and bearded)
1 cup Parmesan cheese (freshly grated)
2 ½ cups bread crumbs
1 cup parsley (freshly chopped)
1 tbsp. chervil (freshly chopped)
3-4 cloves garlic (minced)
2 tsp. basil (freshly chopped)
1 cup olive oil
½ cup white wine
½ cup mussel broth
½ tsp. sea salt
½ tsp. black pepper (freshly ground)
2 lemons (wedged)

Wash the mussels and remove the little beards and the barnacles. Steam the mussels until they are all open and save the broth. Allow the broth to cool. Discard the unopened mussels. Remove one of the shells and place the mussels on a cookie sheet. Blend the parsley, garlic, basil, chervil, and the olive oil in a food processor. Add the mussel broth and the white wine and process a little more. Remove to a glass bowl and fold in the bread crumbs and Parmesan cheese. Cover the mussels in their shells and brown under a broiler. Serve with the lemon wedges. (Serves 8)

Cranky's Fruits of the Sea

16 oysters
16 cherrystone clams
16 mussels
lemon wedges
8 ozs. Cranky's Majestic Cocktail Sauce
3-4 ozs. fresh horseradish
16 slices of cocktail rye (lightly buttered)

Scrub and beard the mussels. Steam the mussels, discard one of the shells and chill. Shuck the oysters and clams just before serving. Place the oysters, clams and mussels on cracked ice in soup bowls and serve with the Cranky's Majestic Cocktail Sauce, lemon wedges, fresh horseradish and the rye slices. (Serves 8)

Cranky's Mussels in Herbs

48 mussels
1 pound butter (sweet)
½ tsp. Cranky's Seafood Seasoning Salt
1 tsp Cranky's Fines Herbes
1 cup white wine

Scrub the mussels and remove the beards. Melt the butter and whisk in the seasoning salt and the fines herbes. Let it stand for 1-2 hours. Place the mussels in a steamer and pour the white wine over them. Melt the herb butter and pour this over the mussels. Cover the pot and steam until all of the mussels are open. Discard the unopened mussels before serving. (Serves 8)

Cranky's Coquille St. Jacques

2 pounds bay scallops
1 cup butter
¼ cup lemon juice
1 tbsp. shallots (finely chopped)
1 cup mushrooms (thinly sliced)
1 cup white wine
2 cups Cranky's Cream Sauce I or II
2 egg yolks (beaten)

1 cup heavy cream
1 cup Parmesan cheese (freshly grated)
2 lemons (wedged)
8 slices of toast (trimmed and made into toast points)
2 tsp. parsley (freshly chopped)
Sea salt to taste
Black pepper to taste (freshly ground)

Drain the scallops and save the liquor. Poach the scallops in the butter and lemon juice and remove from the heat. Separate the scallops into 8 different large scallop shells. Cook the mushrooms and the shallots in the butter and the lemon juice. Add the scallop liquor and the white wine to the pan and season to taste with the salt and the pepper. Simmer until the liquid is reduced to half. Heat the cream sauce and blend in the mushroom and shallot mixture. Beat the eggs in a separate bowl, adding the heavy cream. Whisk the cream and egg mixture into the simmering pan slowly, whisking constantly to keep it from sticking. Continue until the sauce is smooth and creamy. Ladle the sauce over the scallops and sprinkle some cheese on top. Place under the broiler until lightly browned, place the toast points into the sauce on each shell and serve with a lemon wedge. (Serves 8)

Cranky's Herbal Omelet

1 cup finely chopped fresh spinach
½ cup parsley (freshly chopped)
2 tbsp. chives (freshly chopped)
2 tbsp. basil (freshly chopped)
2 tbsp. dill (freshly chopped)
2 tbsp. onion (minced)
2 tbsp. red radishes (minced)
6 tbsp. water
12 eggs (beaten)
½ cup vegetable oil

Combine the spinach, herbs, onion and the red radish. Beat the eggs in a food processor, add the water and the herbs and process quickly. Pour the mixture in a preheated cookie sheet and bake in 350 degree oven until the top is a light brown. Remove from the oven, cut into portions and serve immediately. (Serves 8)

Cranky's Lobster Quiche

3 cups lobster meat
4 tbsp. white dry vermouth
4 tbsp. parsley (freshly chopped)
1 recipe Cranky's Basic Pie Crust
10-12 eggs (depending on the size)
3 cups milk
¼ tsp. cayenne pepper (freshly ground)
¼ tsp. paprika

Chop the lobster meat relatively fine and place in a stainless bowl. Add the dry vermouth and the parsley. Line two pie plates with the pie crust after you have rolled it out so that it is about one eighth of an inch thick. Chill the pie pans with the crust. Brush the pastry with some of the beaten egg whites from two of the eggs. Beat the rest of the eggs in a food processor and add the milk and cayenne pepper. Pour into the bowl that contains the lobster mixture. Separate this mixture into the two pastry shells, dust with the paprika and bake at 450 degrees for 10 minutes … turn the oven to 350 degrees and bake for another 20-25 minutes or until the custard is set and a test knife comes out clean. (Serves 8)

Cranky's Crab Quiche

Follow the same recipe, just substitute lump crab meat for the lobster meat. (Serves 8)

Cranky's Shrimp Quiche

Follow the same recipe, just substitute shrimp for the lobster meat. (Serves 8)

Cranky's Oyster Quiche

Follow the same recipe, just substitute shrimp for the lobster meat. (Serves 8)

Cranky's Scallop Quiche

1 ½ pounds bay scallops
2 tbsp. white dry vermout2 tbsp. parsley (freshly chopped)
1 tsp. thyme (freshly chopped)
½ tsp. sea salt
½ tsp. black pepper (freshly ground)
1 recipe Cranky's Basic Pie Crust
6 eggs (lightly beaten)
1 cup light cream
¼ paprika

Rollout the pastry dough and make 2 rounds that are about one eighth inch thick. Line a pie pan with one of the rounds and fill with the scallop mixture. Place the scallops in the pie dough and sprinkle the scallops with the vermouth, parsley, thyme, salt and the black pepper. Mix the eggs and the cream together and pour over the scallops. Place the other pastry round on top and, using a fork … crimp the edge and then poke some holes in the top of the pie. Bake in a 450 degree oven for 10-12 minutes … reduce the oven temperature to 325 degrees and bake for 25 minutes more or until the quiche is done. (Serves 8)

Cranky's Bay Scallops in Button Mushrooms

48 button mushrooms
48 bay scallops
1 cup white wine
1 cup Cranky's Clarified Butter
2 cloves garlic (minced)
1 tsp. curry
1 tsp. tarragon fresh chopped)
1 tsp. chives (freshly chopped)
1 tsp. parsley (freshly chopped)
¼ tsp. cayenne pepper
1 cup half and half or heavy cream
1 cup Parmesan cheese (freshly grated)
2 lemons (wedged)

Soak the mushrooms in water, remove the stems and save them in the refrigerator for another recipe. Place the mushrooms in a large glass bowl with the wine, curry, tarragon, chives, parsley and the cayenne pepper. Place a weight on top of the mushroom to keep them submerged, and then refrigerate them for 4 hours. Remove the mushrooms from the marinade and place them hollow side up on a cookie sheet. Place a scallop in each mushroom. Pour the marinade into a sauce pan and add the butter and the garlic and bring to a simmer and reduce to about two thirds. Add the half and half or the heavy cream and continue to simmer until smooth and thick. When the desired thickness, spoon over the scallops. Sprinkle the cheese over the tops and broil under a hot broiler until the cheese is light or golden brown. (Serves 8)

Cranky's Czarina's Eggs

Mother Nature has given all of her many creatures the perfect food in a sterilized medium for the betterment of all living things. Although the main purpose is for the propagation of the species, in many cases the egg is a very important link in the food chain, not to mention its worth in the kitchens of mankind. Therefore, I have decided that it doesn't make a difference whether the chicken or the egg came first ... what is of greater importance is which came first ... the egg or the soufflé! I have chosen to accept the first puzzle and leave the solving or handling of such affairs in the capable hands of Mother Nature and to spend my time and energy creating interesting recipes that do justice to the humble egg ... Good scrambling!

½ pound butter (room temperature)
24 eggs (poached)
24 pieces toast (trimmed)
2-4 ozs. anchovy paste
2 cups Cranky's Hollandaise Sauce
3-4 ozs. Beluga caviar (fresh)

Spread the buttered toast with the anchovy paste and place a poached egg on each slice. Cover with hollandaise sauce and top with a small dollop of fresh caviar. (Serves 8-12)

Cranky's Scramblers

16 eggs (beaten)

4 ozs. half and half
1 tbsp. sugar
sea salt to taste
black pepper to taste (freshly ground)
2 cups Cranky's Salsa Rosa
24 sausage links
3 tbsp. butter

Beat the eggs and add the half and half, the sugar, the salt and the black pepper. Brown the sausage links, and then transfer them to a heated platter. Pour off the grease, with the exception of a teaspoonful in the pan. Add the butter to the pan and melt it ... add the scrambled eggs and cook on the soft side. Portion the eggs on heated platters with the sausage on the side and the salsa on top of the eggs. (Serves 8)

Cranky's Buckingham Eggs

During the Seventeenth Century, a gentle by name of George Villiers, the Duke of Buckingham, was quite the about town. Nearly every night he could be seen either at the theatre, dining at the Tour D'Argent in Paris, or in one of the many clubs that he belonged to on both sides of the English Channel. It is said that he entertained on a nightly basis and was famous for light snacks and interesting dishes into the wee hours of the morning. Here is a recipe that has been named after the Duke and truly is a delicious appetizer or after theatre snack.

16 slices of toast (trimmed, eight pieces cut diagonally)
2 tbsp. butter
5-6 tsp. anchovies
16 eggs (well beaten)
6 tbsp. heavy cream
¼ tsp. sea salt
¼ tsp. black pepper (freshly ground)
2-3 tbsp. sharp Cheddar cheese (grated)
1 medium onion (minced)
½ tsp, Worcestershire sauce
2 tsp. mustard (dry)
2-3 ozs. white wine
1 oz. fresh Beluga caviar

Blend the butter, anchovies and the mustard in a bowl and spread on the eight full slices. Beat the eggs and add the cream salt, pepper and minced onion. Melt some butter in a skillet and just before it bubbles, pour in the egg mixture. Stir with a wooden spoon until the mixture starts to thicken. The eggs should have the consistency of loosely scrambled eggs. Mound the eggs up on the anchovy toast that you have put on a warmed dinner plate. Sprinkle them with the grated cheese. Dot each egg portion with a small pat of butter, sprinkle a dash of Worcestershire sauce on each one and place them under the broiler until the cheese melts. Place a dab of caviar on each one and serve at once with a couple of toast points. This little taste delight goes well with a dry white wine chilled vodka or chilled aquavit. (Serves 8)

Cranky's Russian Eggs

3 dz. hard boiled eggs
1 oz. Beluga or Sevruga caviar
1 can anchovies
1 ½ cups Cranky's Hot German Potato Salad (chilled)
1-2 cups Cranky's Classic Mayonnaise
2 tsp. chives (fresh)
2 tsp parsley (fresh)
2 tsp. dill (fresh)
2 tsp. oregano (fresh
2 cups Cranky's Tartar Sauce
1-2 heads Romaine lettuce

Peel the eggs, slice them in half and separate the whites from the yellows. On a large serving platter, place 36 balls of the German potato salad, made with a small ice cream scoop, on a bed of the lettuce. Make a small dent in the potato salad balls with the back of the ice cream scoop. Place the egg yolks and the mayonnaise, along with the parsley, dill, oregano and chives in a food processor and blend until creamy, correcting the seasoning to your taste. Place the egg halves on the potato salad balls. Put the egg yolk mixture in a pastry tube and squeeze enough into each egg white half. Place a dollop of tartar sauce, topped with a small slice of anchovy and a small dollop of caviar. (Serves 8)*

You can use Lumpfish Caviar or Salmon Caviar, if so disposed!

Cranky's Soused Mackerel

4 mackerel (cleaned with the heads removed)
2 spanish onions (sliced)
1 tsp. thyme (freshly chopped)
2 bay leaves (crushed)
½ tsp black pepper (freshly ground)
1 tsp sea salt
2 carrots (finely chopped)
1 tbsp. olive oil
1 qt. white wine
3 tsp. lemon juice

Place the mackerel in a shallow glass baking dish and cover with all of the rest of the ingredients. Put the dish in a 275 degree oven for about 2 hours or until the vegetables are tender. Baste the mixture frequently. Let the mackerel cool in the juices. Place in the refrigerator and serve chilled. This is a marvelous little appetizer. (Serves 8)

Cranky's Escargots à la Bourguignonne

Snails have been eaten by the Romans centuries before the French. The tenderest of snails are harvested at the end of the winter or in the very early spring. They hibernate during the winter and are not likely to have any poisonous toxins from their diet that might be injurious to the diner. Even so, they should be starved for a couple of days so that they purge themselves of these toxins. I like to soak them in a solution of water, sea salt, vinegar and flour. Salt and vinegar tends to disgorge them and the flour fattens them. I then wash them in cold water, blanch them in boiling water, and rinse them in white wine, chicken stock and fines herbs for about 2½–3 hours. They are now at the ready state that they would be in a can. The difference is that they have no preservatives that always have to be rinsed when you used the canned item.

4 ozs. Burgundian snails
1 lb. butter (softened)
3 tbsp. shallots (finely chopped)
¼ tsp. sea salt
1 oz. Worcestershire sauce

3-4 tbsp. bread crumbs
4 dz. large snail shells
2 cloves garlic (freshly minced)
2 tbs. parsley (freshly chopped)
¼ tsp. nutmeg (freshly ground)
¼ tsp. black pepper (freshly ground)
Light dry wine

Wash and drain the snails and the shells. Make some snail butter by blending all of the ingredients together except the white wine. Pour a small amount of the wine into each shell. Place a small amount of snail butter into each shell, followed by one of the washed and rinsed snails. Cover the snail with a generous amount of the snail butter. Dust with some of the bread crumbs. Put 6 snails on a snail dish and pour 1 ounce of wine in each dish. Place in a very hot oven for approximately 10-15 minutes. Serve piping hot with French bread or garlic bread. (Serves 8)

Cranky's Snails alla Romana

The French will certainly argue the point, but I sincerely believe that the Romans were enjoying snails long before the Cultural Revolution in France. On St. John's Eve, when thousands of people flock in front of the famous St. Peter's Basilica, the taste treat of the day has always been snails, bread and good Frascati wine. This has been an annual festival dating back before the dawn of Christianity and certainly pre-dating France as a country. Snails are eaten in great quantities by most of the revelers and are unceremoniously washed down with the golden Frascati wine.

20 snails per person (small snails)
3 tsp. olive oil
½ tsp. basil (freshly chopped)
½ tsp. oregano (freshly chopped)
1 tsp. Italian parsley (freshly chopped)
1 clove garlic (finely minced)
½ cup onion (finely chopped)
4 ozs. tomatoes (crushed and seeded)
½ tsp. ginger (thinly sliced)

Clean and rinse the snails as always. The ingredients listed are for 20 snails so multiply accordingly with the exception of the olive oil. In a large skillet put in the olive oil and get it hot. Put the snails, onions, garlic and herbs in the pan and shake the pan well. After about 2-3 minutes or when the snails are cooked to your taste, add the tomatoes and simmer for about 20-25 minutes. Season the mixture with the salt and pepper and serve piping hot with a lot of garlic bread. (Serves 8)

Cranky's Gefilte Fish ... A Family Secret

Jewish fish cookery probably originated in the areas of Czechoslovakia, Poland and Hungary where there are little or no salt water shorelines resulting in seafood recipes that are devoted to the fresh water species. Gefilte fish is usually made from carp, whitefish or walleye and can be traced back to the early sixteenth century. In a five volume work written by Jan Dubravius entitled, "About the Fish Ponds and Fish Lining Therein", it is stated that over 450,000 acres of breeding ponds for carp and whitefish were a going business in Moravia and Bohemia around 1547, the year that his work was written. I happened to have learned this recipe from Jennie Grossinger while working in her kitchen in the Catskills and I now pass it on to you for your enjoyment. One rule must be followed in the making of great gefilte fish ..."There are no short cuts ... the key is in the chopping of the fish ... if not done as explained in this recipe, the fish balls will come out like rubber balls." Remember to tell your fishmonger that you need the heads and the tails and the bones of the filleted fish to make a broth. The fish must be properly and completely scaled and washed before filleting Also, the weight of the fillets must be made up of tail pieces only without the skins and without any bones. The body part of the fillets can be frozen and used for a delightful meal, after they are properly boned and cooked with your favorite recipe ... the fillets should be used within a week or two to protect from freezer burn or freezer taste.

Approximately 10 pounds fish heads, skins and bones
6 pounds whitefish fillets
6 pounds walleye fillets
7 medium onions
4 celery stalks with leaves
10 carrots
2-3 cups water (ice cold)
4 eggs

2 tbsp. matzo meal
1 tsp. sea salt
1 tsp. black pepper (freshly ground)
2 tbsp. parsley (freshly chopped).
2 tbsp carrots (grated)
1 cup horseradish (fresh)
2-3 heads of Boston lettuce
4 lemons (wedged)

Put the bones, heads and skins of the fish in a large pot, saving one or two of the skins for later use. Bring to a boil and turn to a simmer and simmer for about 5-6 hours, making a wonderful fish consommé. Cut the carrots, celery and onions into chunk size pieces and add them to the pot. Simmer this mixture for about 1 to 1 ½ hours. Pass the fish fillets and the remaining onions through a meat grinder into a large glass bowl. Add the eggs the matzo meal, sea salt and black pepper. This mixture must be chopped in order to get the proper amount of air into the mixture which is the real secret of great Gefilte fish. It takes approximately 35-40 minutes of chopping with a large chef's knife. During the time of chopping, add the cold water slowly ... this will make the texture much lighter and very fluffy. Roll the mixture into balls 1 ½- 2 inches in diameter or whatever size you desire. At this time, put the extra pieces of skin into the broth and place the balls carefully into the simmering pot with a slotted spoon. Cook slowly for about 2 hours on very low heat ... this should reduce the amount of liquid by about half. If it has reduced more than this, you are cooking the balls quicker than you should. Remove the balls from the broth and place in a glass bowl. Strain the broth through a fine sieve and set aside. Gefilte fish can be served hot or cold but most people prefer it cold. I like to serve it on a bed of lettuce. Garnished with parsley, carrots and the jellied broth scooped into balls, the horseradish and lemon wedges. To preserve the fish balls. Pour the broth over them and it will congeal in about 4-6 hours and keep for a long time. (Makes about 60-70 fish balls depending on the size.)

Cranky's Seafood Guacamole

There are thousands of ways to prepare guacamole, but, I truly believe that this is the tastiest on this planet or any other planet.

4 avocados (ripe but not blackened on the inside)
1 cup seafood of your choice (clams, oysters, shrimp, crabmeat, etc. (chopped finely)
4 ounces clam juice
2 medium tomatoes (peeled, seeded and chopped finely but not minced)
1 cup sour cream
4 tbsp. lemon juice (freshly squeezed)
4 green onions (greens and all, roots removed)
8-10 chives
1 tsp. sea salt
1 tsp. black pepper (freshly ground)
1-3 dashes of Worcestershire sauce
3-4 tsp. Cranky's Salsa Verde
1 head of Boston lettuce
1 very large bowl of tortilla chips

Peel and pit the avocados and place everything but the lettuce, the seafood, the tomatoes and the tortilla chips in the food processor and blend until creamy. Place into a glass bowl that is lined with lettuce and fold in the chopped tomatoes. Finally fold in the chopped seafood of choice. Cover with saran wrap and chill for two to three hours before serving. Serve with the room temperature tortilla chips. (Serves about 8-12 Guests)

Cranky's Welsh Rarebit or Cranky's Welsh Rabbit

That's right! Welsh Rarebit. Although commonly spelled Welsh Rabbit and referred to, in this manner, in most cookbooks and by most cookbook authors and food critics and readers, I would like to educate you in my own silly fashion. When King John ruled England during the Crusades, in the absence of the true king, Richard the Lionhearted, who had left England to go to the Crusades, it had become a criminal offense to poach game on the king's land by anyone other than the king and his appointed henchmen. The sad part was that he owned all of the land ... hence, all of the wild game on the land was his or his nobles wild game ... very much like today! The offense was punishable by death, but death never deters the starving man or his family. King John was a greedy man, made greedy by the lords around him, and taxed to people to such an extent that they had very little to put on the table, having had to sell their livestock to pay the taxes. Hence, they would resort to poaching the wild game in the surrounding area, just for their very survival. Some of the local farmers, tradesmen and shopkeepers ... all owing allegiance to the king ... gathering one evening to discuss their lot, were quietly eating their evening meal ... a meal made of bread, cheese and beer ... heated and poured over some stale bread, when they were attacked and arrested by the sheriff's men and brought immediately before the magistrate. The charge was the killing and eating of some of his majesty's wild game ... that being rabbit. The magistrate asked one of the accused what manner of dish it was and was informed that it was called "Welsh Rabbit." The magistrate, not wishing to be unfair due to the fact that he was in the minority, asked if he may taste of the dish. A messenger was sent back to the farmer's house and the dutiful wife brought a piping hot portion to the court. The magistrate thanked the wench and, upon tasting of her fare, he proclaimed, "This is not rabbit ... however, it is a very rare bit!"

16 slices of toast (trimmed)
2 tbsp. butter (melted)
1 cup onions (chopped)
1 cup mushroom caps (thinly sliced)
2 pounds sharp Cheddar cheese
2 cups beer (preferably dark)
2 egg yolks (beaten)
1 tsp. paprika
1 tsp. mustard (dry)
2 pinches cayenne pepper
2 tsp. Worcestershire sauce

Cut 8 slices of toast diagonally in half. Sauté the onions and the mushrooms and place them in a double boiler. Add the butter and the cheese and stir with a wooden spoon. Gradually add the beer that is at room temperature. Stir the mixture slowly, for melted cheese and butter are gentle lovers. Stir the mixture ever so gently until smooth and creamy add the onions and the mushrooms and again stir gently. Now comes the fun part. Slowly, and I do mean slowly, add the well beaten egg yolks while stirring in a slow, constant rhythm. Season the concoction with the rest of the ingredients, stirring constantly. Pour the elixir over the warmed bread in heated dishes garnished with the toast points. Eat quickly ... the sheriff's men are on the way! (Serves 8)

Cranky's Oyster Welsh Rarebit or Rabbit

Welsh Rarebit Recipe
2 cups oysters (freshly shucked and drained)
1 cup onion (finely chopped)

Follow the regular Welsh Rarebit recipe and just before the mixture becomes completely smooth, add the oysters and cook for about 3-4 minutes or until the cheese is smooth. (Serves 8)

Cranky's Scotch Rarebit or Rabbit

This is the same recipe as Welsh Rarebit or Rabbit, with one exception. The Scotch butter their toast. While in Scotland, one of the locals told me that the reason that they butter their toast was to make the Welsh appear more penny pinching then the Scots!

Cranky's English Rarebit or Rabbit

1-2 loaves bread
1 cup Cranky's Hot Like Hell Mustard
2 qts. red wine or ale or stout
3-4 pounds sharp Cheddar cheese
½ tsp paprika

Fill the rarebit plates with a ½ inch slice of bread that has been spread with the mustard. Pour in about ½ cup of wine or ale of choice. Lay strips of the cheese on the bread, enough to cover the bread. Place under the broiler or in a 400 degree oven until the cheese starts to bubble and brown lightly. Remove from the oven or the broiler, dust with the paprika and serve at once. (Serves 8)

Cranky's Rarebit or Rabbit

TO THE ABOVE RECIPE FOR WELSH RAREBIT OR RABBIT … ADD:
2 cups onions (finely chopped)
2 cups mushroom caps (thinly sliced)
2 tbsp. butter

Sauté the onions and mushrooms in butter. Place these items in the top of a double boiler and follow the instructions for Welsh Rarebit or Rabbit. (Serves 8)

Cranky's Salmon Terrine

3 pounds of fresh salmon (boned, skinned and chopped)
6 egg whites
2-3 tsp. sea salt
1 tsp black pepper (freshly ground)
¼ tsp. cayenne pepper (ground)
7-8 cups Cranky's Crème Fraiche
2-3 salmon steaks (skinned and boned)
3 tbsp. parsley (freshly chopped)
3 tbsp. chervil (freshly chopped)
3 tbsp. chives (freshly chopped)
1 tbsp. tarragon (freshly chopped)
3-4 cups Cranky's Green Mayonnaise
1-2 Heads of Boston lettuce

Place the chopped salmon in a food processor along with the egg whites, salt, pepper and cayenne pepper. Purée well. Force the mixture through a fine sieve, discarding the salmon that doesn't go through … this should not be very much. Put the salmon mixture in a glass or stainless steel bowl set in another bowl with cracked ice. Beat in the crème fraiche, 2 or 3 tablespoons at a time until the mousse is very fluffy. Spread half of the mixture in an oiled 3 quart terrine and lay the salmon steaks on top. Make sure that the steaks are devoid of skin, oil layer (the brownish layer that is next to the skin) and any bones whatsoever. Sprinkle the steaks with the parsley, chives, chervil and tarragon. Fill the terrine with the rest of the mixture of mousse. Place the terrine in a deep baking pan and fill that pan up to the same level as the mixture in the terrine … do not let the terrine float. Bake the terrine for 40-45 minutes at 350-375 degrees. Remove the terrine from oven and the water, let it cool and chill overnight, it will shrink from the side of the pan. Remove from the pan and chill for about 2 hours. Slice and serve on beds of lettuce of choice with some green mayonnaise. (Serves 8)

Cranky's Hushpuppies

Most think that hushpuppies are just corn fritters. Well you are wrong. These delightful little snacks were originally made by the cook of the estate for the Master of the Hounds wherever there was a culture that endorsed fox hunting. The Master of the Hounds would have smaller ones fried to keep the hounds at bay before the hunt and the larger ones to feed the hounds at the end of the hunt in order to keep them quiet ... this was their reward. To my knowledge they were fried in bacon grease which you would think, would only make the hounds more excited. I came across this recipe in New Orleans, while dining at K-Paul's, owned by Paul Prudhomme, the ex chef of the Commander's Palace in New Orleans, and it certainly made me howl!

2 cups cornmeal
1 cup flour
1 cup corn flour
2 tbsp baking powder (fresh)
1 ½ tsp. cayenne pepper
1 tsp. black pepper (freshly ground)
1 tsp sea salt
1 tsp. thyme leaves (freshly chopped)
½ tsp white pepper
½ tsp. oregano (freshly chopped)
1 cup green onions (freshly chopped)
3 tsp. garlic (freshly minced)
4 eggs well beaten
2 cups milk
4 tbs. chicken fat or bacon drippings
3-4 cups Cranky's Majestic Cocktail Sauce

Combine all of the dry ingredients in a spacious bowl. Blend in the green onions, thyme, oregano and the garlic. Add the eggs and blend everything together. Brink the milk and the bacon drippings to a boil and take off the stove. Add this to the dry mixture one fourth at a time and mix well between each addition. After all is mixed well, place in the refrigerator to cool for about 1 ½ to 2 hours. In a deep fryer or a large deep frying pan, melt your cooking oil or just use vegetable oil. Drop the batter into the oil one teaspoon at a time, but do not crowd the fryer. Cook until dark golden brown and remove each in it s order. This same recipe can be used to make corn fritters, clam fritters, clam cakes, crab fritters or shrimp fritters or any other kind of fritter. Any of the seafood fritters, are especially good and can be served as a side dish with just about any entrée or soup, especially if they are served with served with Cranky's Majestic Cocktail Sauce or even a salad dressing or BBQ Sauce of your choice. (Makes 50-60 Hushpuppies

The Early History of Soup-Maybe!!!

In one of the many ancient corners where cook lore lurks, there is a story about the first soup made by mankind and makes a certain amount of nonsense ... According to the folklore, there was a tribal chief by the name of Ugliar. On a cold wintry morning, he decided that to wash was rather unpleasant. The water seemed to change in density and bruised the skin and when shaving with an icicle, the edge would get dull and cause an abrasive rash to form.

This had to be remedied and it wasn't until one of his tribesmen suggested that they build a fire under the stone that caught the water and this might make it more pleasant to the touch. You have to realize that Ugliar's tribe, the Ugliers, were industrious people and far ahead of their time, already having discovered fire, and were presently trying to solve the age old problem of which was better ... the square or the round wheel.

On a crisp clear fall morning, Ugliar threw some wood on the fire and noticed that the water stone next to the fire was full to the brim. "Ti tsum evah deniar tsai thgin," which translated means, "It must have rained last night."

He decided to clean up a bit before his tribe arose from their beauty sleep which they all dearly needed. Low and behold, he noticed that the hard water in the stone was becoming soft and warm. He decided that this was definitely caused by the fire and reminded himself to reward his ingenious tribesman for the suggestion.

All of the sudden, a treefruit fell from the branch overhanging the mouth of the cave. Ugliar noticed that his caused bubbles to rise in the water. He watched for a while, finally thrusting his finger in the water. Yelping, he pulled his hand out of the boiling water and stuck it in his mouth. This soothed his throbbing finger but, to his surprise the water tasted sweeter.

Ugliar got a brilliant idea. Running over to the well picked carcasses of a past meal, he wrenched a small rib bone from the bleached skeleton of a baby mastodon. Starting to stir the stone cauldron, he attracted a great deal of attention from his fellow tribesmen.

"Gnirb em emos sffutsdoof ot hcihw uoy evah ssecca, ti lliw ekam eht retaw etsat retteb." Translated this means, "Bring me some foodstuffs to which you have access, it will make the water taste better.

One brought an onion, another a saber tooth tiger's tongue, still another brought two large heads of what appeared to be cabbage. All afternoon while Ugliar stirred the water, his tribesmen donated various items to the pot ... a bird here, a bat there, three or four lizards, more red treefruits and other green, yellow and orange objects ... many hooves, numerous ears and tails and an occasional chunk of meat.

All this time, Ugliar lovingly stirred and stirred until the fire subsided but never went out and the water was thick with cooked objects of all sorts. A strange but pleasant aroma hovered over the campfire and permeated the very inner recesses of the cave.

The tribesmen gathered round the fire and after Ugliar took his regal portion, they helped themselves. Grunts of enjoyment and belches of fulfillment crackled the crisp fall dusk. Almost in unison they changed, "Puoswets, Ugliar! Puoswets, Ugliar! Puoswets, Ugliar!" long into the night.

Ugliar remained the tribal chief until the ripe old age of seventy eight years old, loving many wives, siring hundreds of beautiful daughters and strong sons, but never did he give his secret to his tribe nor share it with his rivals. Most men of thinking attribute his long life and great lovemaking ability to the soup, but that is for you to decide.

On his deathbed, he summoned his oldest and strongest son to his side. Weakly he beckoned his son to approach and place his ear close to him so that he might here his father's last words.

"Uoy era eht redael fo eht ebirt won dna I evig siht tib fo esivda. Taert ruoy seviw ylgnivol, hceat ruoy nerdlihc thgir morf gnorw, egduj ruoy nemebirt ylriaf, tub reven reve evig eht epicer rof puoswets ot enoyna tpecxe ruoy rieh. Translated this should be a lesson to us all. "Treat your wives lovingly, teach your children right from wrong, judge your tribesmen fairly, but never, ever give the recipe for Stewsoup to anyone except our heir."

As a result of this sage advice, some recipes have been passed from king to prince, chef to cook, father to son, mother to daughter, but never to the next door neighbor. It is the very secret of the hearth.

Over the centuries, poets have rhymed the wonders of soup, minstrels have strummed and warbled the notes of great flavor, and a poem was even written by Mery about Bouillabaisse and I must agree with all of their accolades.

Not even love warms the heart, body, and soul like a hearty bowl of soup on a cold wintry night. Although a fine bowl of soup will never replace love's ecstasy, it will nourish the bodies of the young, help cure the sick, warm the frostbitten, take the chill out of your bones and, in general, rekindle the first of mankind giving great comfort to both young and old on a damp, dark, overcast day of which we have far too many to contend with in our lives.

I have tried to include in this chapter the soups that cure some of the maladies of mankind that our ancestors and their wonderful searching for the truth, the curious and the new have left for our enjoyments.

It includes soups, bouillons and broths made from fish and fowl, meat and vegetable, wild game and rice, and even fruit and nuts … some hot, some cold, and some jellied.

I trust you will find your favorites and explore the new and different. Although they will never replace love, a good soup might give you the strength and the courage to carry on with style and vigor. In sincerely believe that most of these recipes will satisfy your particular needs … at least for a short time.

STEWS AND SOUPS

The average peasant household normally served dishes that contained great volumes of inexpensive, but tough cuts of meat with lots of vegetables cheaply and readily obtainable. Many of these soups are so thick that a spoon plunged into the bowl easily stands on end. What is wonderful about these concoctions is that the leftovers can be normally placed in a casserole over bread and baked for a short while for the next day's lunch. Some of the common vegetables found in many of these combination soup/stews were cabbages, potatoes, beans, turnips, beets, carrots, onions, celery, etc. I have always enjoyed trying the local fare when traveling and have never felt as though I was dining on cheap food. In fact I have always felt that I was partaking in traditional fare that was both deeply satisfying and gastronomically enlightening. I have, however, separated soups from stews giving stews their very own chapter along with meat and fish pies.

Cranky's Smoked Mussel Soup

This is a taste delight that would satisfy even the despotic czars of Russia, who had a tendency to lop off the heads of the kitchen staff if the meal didn't meet with their approvals. Most of the colder areas of the world were into smoking and freezing long before the rest of the world, and this recipe is a result of those times.

24-36 fresh mussels (scrubbed and bearded)
4 tbsp green onions (finely chopped with roots removed)
4 tbsp butter
1 qt. water
2 cups Cranky's Béchamel Sauce
1 ½ heavy cream
2 tbsp parsley (freshly chopped)
2 tsp. paprika
8 squares of butter

You can buy smoked mussels in a good seafood market, however, or you smoke your own very simply. Steam the mussels, remove from the shells and place on a piece of aluminum foil in your covered barbeque grill, add some soaked hickory chips or maple chips to the hot coals. This takes about 30 minutes. They can then be used at once or frozen for later use. In a large saucepan, sauté the green onions in some butter, and add the saved mussel broth after it is strained. Stir in the Béchamel sauce, and when the soup is heated, add the mussels. Bring to a boil and reduce by one fifth. Swirl in the heavy cream and thicken the soup to the desired consistency. Serve the soup piping hot, garnishing with the paprika and parsley with a square of utter in the middle of each serving. Season the soup to your personal taste. (Serves 8)

Cranky's Turtle Soup

2 pounds turtle meat (fresh if possible and cut into bite size pieces)
4 qts. water
4 medium onions (chopped)
2 bay leaves
½ tsp. cayenne pepper
1 tsp. sea salt
½ tsp. white pepper

½ cup butter
½ cup flour
½ cup Cranky's Tomato Purée
1 tbs. Worcestershire sauce
1 cup Cranky's Chicken Stock
4 hard boiled eggs (chopped)
2-3 tbsp. lemon juice (freshly squeezed)

In a 4 quart kettle, braise the turtle meat. Add the water and bring to a boil. Skim off the foam periodically. Add the onions to the kettle, saving one. Finely chop the last onion and set aside for later. Add the bay leaves, cayenne, white pepper and the salt. Cover and simmer for about 2 hours or until the turtle meat is tender. Remove meat with a slotted spoon and set aside. Strain the broth and set it aside. In the same kettle, melt the butter over medium heat. Sauté the chopped onions until translucent, add the flour, stir until bubbly and lightly browned. Whisk in the Tomato Purée and the Worcestershire sauce. Simmer the mixture, uncovered, for about 10 minutes. Add the chicken stock, eggs, lemon juice and the cooked meat. Simmer until heated through and serve immediately. (Serves 8)

Cranky's Turtle Soup Cajun Style

I came across this recipe in New Orleans at the Commander's Palace and, believe me, it is the real article ... Cajun influence and all. It is rich and robust and will satisfy your every taste bud.

3 pounds turtle meat (fresh, if possible)
4-5 tbsp. butter
2 tbsp olive oil
2 tbsp. vegetable oil
2 tbsp. margarine
5-6 bay leaves
½ tsp. sea salt
1 tsp. white pepper (freshly ground0
1 tsp. cayenne pepper (ground)
4-5 cloves garlic (minced)
1 bunch green onions (root removed, freshly chopped)
3 tsp. thyme (freshly chopped)

1 tsp. dry mustard
2 tsp. whole black peppercorns (crushed)
1 tsp. cumin (ground)
1 pound spinach leaves (finely chopped)
2 large onions (finely chopped)
1 cup celery (finely chopped)
1 qt. Cranky's Tomato Sauce
1 cup flour
3 qts. Cranky's Beef Stock
1 cup parsley (freshly and finely chopped)
1 lemon (juiced)
1 lemon rind (scraped thin)
6 hard boiled eggs (peeled and cut into quarters
2 cups dry sherry

Finely chop the turtle meat with a chef's knife. Take a large earthenware pot and sauté the turtle meat about 6-7 minutes. The combination of the butter, olive oil, vegetable oil and the margarine will not destroy or overwhelm the delicate flavor of the turtle meat. Combine the bay leaves, salt, white pepper, cayenne pepper, garlic, peppercorns, green onions, thyme, mustard, basil and cumin. Stir this into the pot and simmer for about 15 minutes. Add the tomato sauce and simmer for another 10 minutes … stirring constantly. At this time, whisk the flour into the mix, stirring constantly and making sure nothing sticks to the bottom of the pot. Introduce about one half of the beef stock … stir to make sure nothing has stuck to the bottom and then add the rest of the beef stock. Bring to a boil and then simmer for about 35-45 minutes longer, stirring as often as needed. Process the parsley and the lemon rind until minced. Add the hard boiled eggs and process until they are coarsely chopped. Add this to the soup and stir. Swirl in one half the sherry and simmer for another 15 minutes. Stir and remove from the heat. Search for the bay leaves and discard. Salt and pepper to taste and serve piping hot with a side of the remaining sherry. Serves 8-10)

Cranky's Cream of Crab and Avocado Soup

4 large avocados (ripe but not blackened)
1 ½ cups lump crab meat (crushed lightly)
1 dried chili pepper

4 cups Cranky's Chicken Stock
2 cups heavy cream
2 large avocados
1 tsp. sea salt
1 tsp. white pepper (freshly ground)

Peel and mash the avocados with a potato masher. Place the chili pepper, the mashed avocado and the chicken stock in the top of a double boiler. Heat the soup to just under a boil and add the heavy cream, stirring occasionally, and bring back to just under a boil. Peel and pit the other avocados and cut them into bite size pieces. Put them into the soup, add the crab meat, stir for two to three minutes very gently and season with salt and pepper. Ladle gently into warm bowls. (Serves 8)

Cranky's Lobster Minestrone

½ tsp red wine vinegar
8-1 pound live Maine lobsters
2 tbsp. olive oil
2 white onions (finely chopped)
2 garlic cloves (minced)
1 ½ qts. Cranky's Lobster Stock
2 cups navy beans (soaked and rinsed for at least three hours)
2 sweet red pepper (seeded and chopped)
2 sweet green pepper (seeded and chopped)
1 8-10 inch zucchini (seeded and sliced)
1 8-10 inch yellow squash (seeded and sliced)
1 medium egg plant (peeled and diced)
2 tomatoes (peeled, seeded and chopped)
¼ cup basil (freshly chopped)
4 cooked cups angel hair (cooked al dente)
2 cups Cranky's Lobster stock

Boil the lobsters with some salt, red wine vinegar and the dill. When the lobsters are bright red and floating, remove from the water a chill in the refrigerator. Remove the meat from the claws and the tails and cut into bit size pieces and refrigerate. Remove all of the tomalley and the red roe from the body cavities and save in the refrigerator. In a large soup kettle, heat the olive oil and sauté the garlic, onion red pepper and the green pepper until the onions are translucent. Add the first portion of lobster stock to the kettle, along with the bean and simmer for about 25-30 minutes. When the beans are still chewy, add the yellow squash and the zucchini that you have already sautéed and simmer for 10 more minutes. Finally add the last of the lobster stock, the tomatoes, the basil and the salt and pepper to taste. Simmer until the soup starts to thicken and the beans are just right. In a glass bowl, mash up the tomalley and add to the soup along with the lobster pieces. Bring to a fast boil and remove from the stove. Add the pasta and serve at once. (This will serve 8 with enough for seconds … all will want another serving)

Cranky's Beer and Oyster Soup

This is a great and tasty treat for those buddies that come over to your house to watch the football or hockey or basketball games on a cold Sunday afternoon

3 qts. beer, ale or stout of your choice
4 cups water
1 cup sugar
2 sticks cinnamon
4 whole cloves
¼ tsp. sea salt
½ cup cold water
6 tbsp flour
6 egg yolks
1 ½ cups freshly shucked oysters
6 egg whites beaten to peaks
2 lemons (sliced)

In a large saucepan, bring the beer, water, sugar and spices to a boil. In a large stainless bowl, mix the flour to a smooth by adding a little cold water, stir in the egg yolks and when the mixture is smooth, add it to the boiling liquid in the pan. Stirring steadily and quickly, bring everything to a boil again, and add the oysters. Stir for 1-2 minutes and then stir in the egg whites just before serving. Serve with some small pieces of rye bread and float a slice of lemon on the top of each serving. (Serves 8)

Cranky's Manhattan Clam Chowder

This is the richest recipe that I have ever come across for Manhattan Clam Chowder, however it could never be served in a restaurant for the normal price of a bowl of chowder. I find it a lot easier to make a lot of this at one time and then to place it in containers and freeze it for later use.

50-60 large chowder clams or 80-100 cherrystones
4 ozs. salt pork (diced finely)
1 ½ sweet green peppers (finely chopped)
4 large carrots (finely chopped)
3 cups celery (freshly chopped)
4 28 oz. cans crushed tomatoes
1 gallon of water
1 cup Cranky's Tomato Paste
4 cups tomatoes (peeled, seeded and diced)
4 cups potatoes (peeled and diced)
¼ cup Worcestershire sauce
2 tsp. paprika
2 tsp. sea salt
1 tsp. nutmeg (freshly ground)
2–4 bay leaves
2 tsp. black pepper (freshly ground)
2 tsp. mace
2 tsp. thyme (freshly chopped)
2 tsp. oregano (freshly chopped)
4 tsp. parsley (freshly chopped)

Place the clams in a very large put and the water and a handful of salt. Steam until the clams are all open and let the pot cool. In another kettle, sauté the salt pork until translucent and add all of the vegetables and the herbs and spices. When the onions are translucent, add all of the other ingredients with the exception of the potatoes and the clams. Bring to a boil and allow the chowder to simmer until the vegetables are crunchy. While this is going on, remove the clams from the shells and chop them until the pieces are about ¼ inch in size. Put the chopped clams into the chowder along with the clam broth and bring the chowder to a rolling boil for about 10-20 minutes in order to reduce the volume slightly. This will make a much richer chowder. Be careful not to pour the residue from the clam broth into the chowder. After the liquid is reduced a bit, add the potatoes and cook until they are the proper consistency. Your Manhattan clam chowder is done. Allow to cool, stir from the bottom and ladle into Mason jars and seal. Allow to cool. If planning to freeze, do not cover until frozen because of the expansion. (Makes about 6-8 quarts)

Cranky's New England Clam Chowder

24 chowder clams
4 stalks celery with leaves (freshly chopped)
2 medium onion (freshly chopped)
1-2 bay leaves
1 bunch of parsley (freshly chopped)
2 quarts of water
1 cup potatoes (diced)
1 stalk of celery (finely sliced)
2 ozs. salt pork (finely chopped)
2 leeks (split, rinsed and finely chopped)
3-4 tbsp. flour
1-2 tbsp. butter (melted)
2 cups heavy cream
1 tsp paprika
Sea salt to taste
Black pepper to taste (freshly ground)

Wash the clams and steam with the next five ingredients in a large kettle until all are open … will take about 10-15 minutes. Strain the stock into a large sauce pan and throw out the dredges. Keep on a very low simmer. Add the potatoes and cook until tender. Strain the potatoes out of the clam broth and set aside to keep them from overcooking. Remove the steamed clams from the shells, discard the shells and chop the clams to ¼ inch pieces. Set them aside. Slowly, on low heat, sauté the salt pork, onions, celery and the leeks in the kettle. It is not even necessary to wash or rinse or clean it. Simmer for 10-12 minutes or until the salt pork is soft and translucent … then whisk in the flour. Whisk in the clam broth and simmer for about 8-10 minutes. Reduce to 1½-2 quarts. Whisk in the hot cream and thicken and stir until smooth. Add the clams, the butter, the potatoes, the parsley and the paprika and the salt and pepper to taste. Stir until piping hot but not boiling. Serve in warmed bowls and enjoy. (Serves 8)

Cranky's Red Snapper Chowder

1 leek (white and pale green sections only)
1 pound red snapper fillets (bones and chunked to bite size)
1 tsp. sea salt
1 tbsp. olive oil
2 garlic cloves (minced)
1 tsp. coriander (freshly ground)
2 large boiling potatoes (peeled and diced)
1 quart tomatoes (peeled, seeded and crushed)
3 cups Cranky's Fish Stock
1 cup Cranky's Vegetable Stock
2 tbsp. parsley (freshly chopped)
1 small orange (juiced)
½ tsp. orange rind (grated)

Cut the leek into on half inch pieces. Season the snapper with salt and refrigerator. In a large kettle, sauté the leek until softened. Add the garlic, coriander and the cayenne and cook for about 2 minutes. Add the potatoes, tomatoes, fish stock, vegetable stock and the orange juice. Simmer for about 10-15 minutes and stir in the red snapper pieces, parsley and the orange rind. Cook until the red snapper is done and serve in warm bowls. (Serves 8)

Cranky's Florida Keys Conch Chowder

2 pounds conch meat (freshly ground)
2 large onions (chopped)
3 cloves garlic (crushed)
1 sweet green pepper (seeded and finely chopped)
20 ozs. Cranky's Tomato Sauce
4 medium potatoes (peeled and diced)
2 tbsp. oregano (freshly chopped)
1 tsp. sea salt
½ tsp. black pepper (freshly ground)
1 bird pepper (seeded, white parts removed and finely chopped)

2 cups white wine
½ cup parsley (freshly chopped)
¼ tbsp. dill (freshly chopped)
8 oz. dry sherry

Put the conch meat through a meat grinder using a course blade. Cover with water and simmer for about 30 minutes. Add the onions, garlic, green pepper, tomato sauce, tomato paste and the white wine. Add 2-3 cups of water at this time. Simmer for about 30 minutes. Add the potatoes, oregano, salt, pepper and the bird pepper. Simmer until the potatoes are tender. Serve in individual warm bowls with a side ounce of sherry, parsley and dill. (Serves 8)

Cranky's Salmon Chowder

12 ozs. salmon fillet (fresh, boned and chopped coarsely)
½ cup butter
½ sweet green pepper (seeded and finely chopped)
½ cup green onion (finely chopped including the green leaves)
3 tbsp. flour
1 tsp. sea salt
½ tsp. black pepper (freshly ground)
6 cups half and half
1 cup Cranky's Fish Stock or Cranky's Clam Broth
2 tbsp. pimento (finely diced)
2 tbsp. chives (freshly snipped and chopped)

In a large sauce pan, melt the butter and sauté the green pepper, green onions and the celery until the onions are translucent and a light brown. Whisk in the sea salt, pepper and the flour until it is a smooth paste. Cook this for a quick minute. Remove from the heat and add about one cup of half and half. Stir this until smoothly blended. Return to the heat and simmer, stirring constantly until it starts to thicken. Add the rest of the half and half, heat to a simmer point and add the salmon. It is important that you simmer long enough to cook the salmon but without scorching the soup. This is a good time to add the clam broth and the pimento. Heat again and simmer until it is the proper thickness, stirring often. Serve in warm bowls and garnish with some chives. (Serves 8)

Cranky's Authentic Shrimp Creole Gumbo

½ pound bacon (chopped)
1 large onion (sliced)
4 stalks celery (freshly chopped)
3-4 cloves garlic (minced)
1 large sweet green pepper (pitted, seeded and stem removed and chopped)
2 bay leaves (crushed)
3 tbs. parsley (freshly chopped)
½ tsp. sea salt
1 tsp. black pepper (freshly ground)
1-2 tbsp. gumbo file
2 tsp. oregano (freshly chopped)
1 tsp. basil (freshly chopped)
2 tsp. Tabasco sauce
4 qts. water
2 pounds of tomatoes (peeled and seeded and chopped)
1 pound okra (fresh, stems removed and chopped)
1 ½ cups of dry rice
2 pounds of green shrimp (21-25 count raw in the shell)
2 cups oysters (freshly shucked)

Sauté the chopped bacon in a very large soup kettle for 3-4 minutes. In a separate pot, cook the rice and set it aside. To the original kettle add the onion, celery, garlic, green pepper, bay leaves, salt, pepper, gumbo file, oregano, basil, Tabasco sauce and water. Simmer until the celery is half tender. Add the okra and the tomatoes and cook for about 15-18 minutes. Add the cooked rice and let simmer for about 5 minutes. Finally add the shrimp and the oysters along with the oyster liquor and cook for 3 more minutes. Take off of the stove, cover and let set for 10 minutes. Serve in hot bowls. Enjoy. (Serves 8)

Cranky's Raw Oyster Soup

40 live fresh oysters (shucked, saving the liquor)
2 tbsp. chives (freshly chopped)
2 tbsp. tarragon leaves (freshly chopped)
4 tomatoes (peeled, seeded and finely chopped)
8-10 drops of Ricard or Pernod

6 cups heavy cream
2 lemons (wedged)
2 loaves of French bread

Plunge the tarragon leaves in boiling water for 5-10 seconds. Rinse in cold water and place in a large glass bowl. Add the oysters, straining the liquor so that no oyster shell chips get in the mix. Add the chives, tomatoes, Ricard or Pernod and the heavy cream. Mix well, cover and chill for 3-5 hours. Serve with slices of French bread. (Serves 8)

Cranky's Scallop Soup

12-15 sea scallops (fresh)
2 qts. Cranky's Chicken Stock
1 tsp. sea salt
1 tsp. white pepper (freshly ground)
2 egg whites (beaten)
2 ozs. ham (cut into julienne strips)
2 tsp. coriander (freshly minced)
2 tsp. parsley (freshly chopped)
2 lemons (wedged)

Heat the chicken stock in a soup kettle and keep it at a low simmer. Remove the muscles from the sides of the sea scallops and steam them over the broth, allowing the scallop liquor to drip into the broth. Remove the scallops from the heat and slice them, julienne style and set aside. Add all of the other items to the kettle. Simmer for 2-3 minutes, add the slices of scallops and ladle into warm soup bowls. Serve with a1 or 2 lemon wedges. (Serves 8)

Cranky's Billi-Bi Soup

I have to thank Maxim de Paris for the name of this wonderful soup, as well as the name, but Cranky deserves the credit for the secret ingredient that makes this concoction a gourmet's delight. You guessed it ... the Migionettes!

6 dozen large mussels (fresh, washed and the little beards removed)
2 medium onions (finely chopped)
1 cup celery (finely chopped)

1 qt. white wine
½ pound butter
1 qt. Cranky's Fish Stock
1 qt. heavy cream
4tbsp. parsley (finely chopped)
4-6 clusters of fragrant Mignonettes
2 tsp. black pepper (freshly ground)
1 tsp. sea salt
1 cup Parmesan cheese (freshly grated)

Put the mussels in a large steamer along with all of the other ingredients except the heavy cream, the grated cheese and the Mignonettes. When the mussels are all open, discard the ones that are not open, strain the liquid through some fine cheesecloth and reduce to half. While reducing the liquid, take the mussels out of the shells and set aside. When the broth is properly reduces to one half, blend in the heavy cream with a whisk, being sure not to bring the entire liquid to a rolling boil. Simmer and allow the liquid to thicken. Fold in the mussels and bring back to a slow or low simmer. Add the mignonettes, stir for 1-2 minutes and serve in warm bowls with grated cheese on the side for those that have additional adventure genes. (Serves 8)*

Mignonettes ... a plant with particularly fragrant clusters of flowers that are found on the Mediterranean coast. I have found that most of the informed florists can come up with flowers that they have in stock ... rose petals or Hibiscus come to mind ... that are not injurious to the person if they are consumed.

Cranky's Blue Crab Soup with Picada

1 medium onion (finely chopped)
1 carrot (peeled and finely chopped)
1 celery stalk (finely chopped)
2 tbsp vegetable oil
6-8 live blue claw crabs
6-8 large ripe tomatoes (peeled and seeded and chopped)
2 qts. Cranky's Chicken Stock
1 cup Cranky's Sauce Picada
½ tsp. cayenne pepper
1 cup heavy cream

¼ tsp. saffron threads
1 tbsp. white wine

Cook all of the vegetables in the oil in a large soup kettle. While this is going on, hit the crabs until they no longer move with the back of a cleaver or a rolling pin ... do not bust them up. The claws and bodies can be picked clean of the crab meat at a later time. Remove the back flap which releases the top shell from the body of the crabs. Remove the center gall bladder sack behind the eyes in the shell and then scrape all of the tomalley into the kettle. Tear off all of the small legs of the crabs and crush them with the rolling pin and put these into the kettle. Add the tomatoes and the fish stock to the kettle and put a steamer/strainer in the pot and place the crab bodies and the large claws in the steamer/strainer. Cover and simmer for about 10-15 minutes or until the crab bodies are reddish pink. Take the kettle off of the heat and set aside. Pick the meat out of the shells of the crab bodies and the large claws and put in a closable container and freeze for crab cocktail at a latter time. Put all of the resulting shells into the soup kettle and return to the stove and simmer for about one hour ... adding water of necessary. While this is going on soak the saffron in the wine for about 30 minutes. At this time, remove the kettle from the stove and strain the liquid through a very fine sieve or meshed strainer into a clean kettle. Whisk into the liquid three quarters of a cup of the Picada and bring to a simmer. Add the cayenne pepper at this time. Whisk in the remaining Picada and the heavy cream along with the wine and the saffron just before eating. (Serves 8)*

This can be served with slices of toasted French bread on the side or even at the bottom of the bowls.

Cranky's Lobster Bisque

2 qts. Cranky's Fish Stock
2-3 pounds fish heads
2 onions (sliced)
¼ bunch parsley (freshly chopped)
1-2 cloves garlic (minced)
¼ tsp. black peppercorns (freshly ground)
1 tsp. lemon juice
2 qts. water

1 cup dry white wine
¼ cup vegetable or olive oil
2-1½ pound live Maine lobsters
2 stalks celery (diced)
1 medium onion (fresh chopped)
1 large carrot (freshly peeled and chopped)
½ cup flour
1 tsp. paprika
1 ½ tbsp. Cranky's Tomato Purée
Sea salt to taste
Black pepper to taste (freshly ground)
1 cup warm heavy cream
½ cup dry sherry
1 loaf of French bread

Place the fish stock, onions, parsley, garlic, peppercorns, lemon juice, water and the wine in a large kettle and simmer for about 1 hour. Strain through a fine sieve and set aside. In the same kettle bring the cooking oil to high heat and add the chopped tails and cracked claws of the two lobsters. Cook until the shells are bright red. Pick the meat out of the shells and set the meat aside. Chop the cooked shells and the bodies of the lobsters up and return all of the shells, along with the heads, that contain the tomalley into the pot along with the fish stock and simmer for at least 1-2 hours. Add the celery, onion, carrots and the flour. Stir and simmer for 15 minutes. Stir in the paprika, tomato purée, pepper and salt. Cover the kettle and simmer for another 1-2 hours. Strain the broth and throw away the shells. Reduce the broth to at least one half of the volume. (approximately 2 quarts) Dice the lobster meat very finely and swirl into the soup. Warm the heavy cream and gradually stir into the soup. Thicken to your desired consistency and thickness and serve piping hot in warm soup crocks with a side of dry sherry. (Serves 8)

Cranky's Shrimp Bisque

Prepare in the same manner as you would prepare the Lobster Bisque. Simply substitute the shrimp for the lobster ... treating the shells in the same manner as you treated the lobster shells and the heads, however, the shrimp do not and should not have to be cooked as long. (Serves 8)

Cranky's Scallop Bisque

2 qts. Cranky's Fish Stock
4 cups white wine
½ cup celery (chopped)
½ cup carrots (chopped)
2 bay leaves
2 stalks lemon grass (chopped)
2 pounds sea scallops (muscles removed)
¼ cup olive oil
4 cups heavy cream
sea salt to taste
white pepper to taste
2-3 tbsp. chives (fresh snipped and finally chopped)

Place the fish stock, white wine, celery, carrots, onions, bay leaves and lemon grass. Simmer for about 1 hour, strain and reduce to about half. Sear the scallops in the olive oil for about 1-2 minutes on each side. Strain the stock into a saucepan and add the heavy cream, thickening by whisking and simmering for about 20 minutes. Add the scallops that have been drained. I like to slice them in half cross grained. Salt and pepper the soup to taste. Ladle into warm bowls and garnish with the chives. (Serves 8)

Cranky's Maryland Crab Bisque

This is a taste treat that will satisfy and seafood lover. It is rich, creamy and extraordinary.

1 cup onion (finally chopped)
1 cup celery (finally chopped)
1 cup button mushrooms (thinly sliced)
1 cup butter
4 tbsp. flour
½ tsp. white pepper (freshly ground)
2 tsp. paprika
2 cups tomato juice
2 qts. Cranky's Fish Stock
1 tsp chervil (freshly chopped)

1 pound Maryland blue claw crab meat
8 ozs. dry sherry

Sauté the onions and the celery until the onions are translucent. Add the mushrooms and cook for about 2-3 minutes. Whisk in the flour, pepper and the paprika into the butter and then add the tomato juice, stirring as it thickens. Stir in the chervil and cook, stirring constantly on high heat until it is thick and creamy. The best results are achieved if live crabs are used and the stock is made from the shells, but, if you use frozen or canned crabmeat, it can produce excellent results. Bottled clam juice can be used instead of Cranky's Fish Stock. Just before serving, add the crabmeat to the bisque and stir as you heat before serving. A side a dry sherry can be served if you prefer, but it is not necessary. Bon Appetit. (Serves 8)

Cranky's Chilled Salmon Bisque

1 pound of fresh salmon fillets (skinned)
1 clove of garlic (minced)
1 medium onion (finely chopped
2 tbsp. butter
2-3 cups Cranky's Court Bouillon for Fish
3 cups half and half
½ tsp. Tabasco sauce
½ cup dill (freshly and finely chopped)
½ tsp. black pepper (freshly ground)
1 cup heavy cream
4-5 tbsp. dry sherry

Sauté the garlic and the onion in some butter and place the mixture, when the onions are translucent, in a food processor. Poach the salmon in some court bouillon on very low heat. When the salmon is properly poached, remove from the liquid and allow the salmon to cool. Add the salmon to the Tabasco sauce, the half and half, the dill, black pepper and the court bouillon and blend to a froth in your food processor. Force this through a fine sieve. Put this into a glass bowl and stir in the heavy cream and the sherry. You can chill this and serve this delightful taste treat. You can also, serve the sherry on the side. (Serves 8)

Cranky's Clam Broth

This can be served as a soup or used in place of fish stock in any of a thousand recipes without the whipped cream. The steamed clams can be frozen in a plastic container for later use.

2-3 dz. cherrystones
6-7 cups water
1 tbsp. olive oil
4 shallots (coarsely chopped)
3-4 tbsp. parsley (freshly chopped)
½ cup heavy cream (whipped to peaks)

Scrub the clams and place them in a large kettle with a lid along with the water and the olive oil, shallots and the parsley. Simmer until all of the clams are open. Remove the clams from the shells and save for a rainy day in the freezer. Strain the broth through very fine cheesecloth. Heat and serve piping hot in warm cups or bowls with a spoonful of the whipped cream and garnished with some chopped parsley. (Serves 8)

Cranky's Jellied Seafood Consomme

2 cups Cranky's Shrimp Stock
2 cups Cranky's Fish Stock
2 cups scallop juice
2 cups clam juice
Knox gelatin (as needed-follow directions on the package)
2 cups dry sherry
2 lemons (wedged)
2 tbsp. dill (freshly chopped)
2 tbsp. chervil (freshly chopped)
2 tbsp. chives (freshly chopped)
2 lemons (wedged)

Place the shrimp stock, fish stock, scallop juice and clam juice in a soup kettle and reduce the volume by half. Remove from the heat and add the dill, chervil, chives and the gelatin. Add enough of the Knox gelatin according to the instructions on the package. If the fish stock was gelatinous, before you added it to the kettle, you might not need as much. Stir until the gelatin is completely dissolved. Add the sherry to taste and pour into glass molds or a large glass bowl. Serve in small cold soup cups with lemon wedges and chopped parsley. (Serves 8)

Cranky's Bouillabaisse

As I stated before, in this cookbook, Jewish fish cookery, probably originated in the areas of Czechoslovakia, Poland and Hungary. There are little or no salt water shorelines in these countries, resulting in seafood recipes that are devoted to the fresh water species. Gefilte fish is usually made from carp, whitefish or walleye and can be traced back to the early sixteenth century. In a five volume work written by Jan Dubravius entitled, "About the Fish Ponds and Fish Lining Therein", it is stated that over 450,000 acres of breeding ponds for carp and whitefish were a going business in Moravia and Bohemia around 1547, the year that his work was written. I, also, happened to have learned this recipe from Jennie Grossinger while working in her kitchen in the Catskills and I now pass it on to you for your enjoyment. One rule must be followed, saffron is a matter of taste and color intensity ... so let your taste buds and your conscience be your guide. Just like in the making of great Gefilte fish ... there are no short cuts.

2 pounds whole sea robin (grondin)
1 ½ pounds whole conger eel (conger)
1 ½ pounds whole goatfish (rouget)
1 ½ pounds whole rockfish (racasse)
1 ½ pounds whole John Dory (Saint-Pierre)
1 ½ pounds whole codfish (lotte)
1 ½ pounds whole blackfish (vive)
8 whole live 1 pound langoustines
1 ½ olive oil
8 cloves garlic (crushed)
1 large onion (studded with 15 or 20 whole cloves)
1 large onion (chopped)
2 cups carrots, onions and celery (finely chopped)
2 cups celery (chopped)
4 large tomatoes (peeled, seeded, chopped)
2 tsp. thyme (freshly chopped)
1 tsp. parsley (freshly chopped)

2-3 bay leaves
1 orange rind
2 ozs. fennel (minced)
½ tsp. sea salt
½ tsp. white pepper (freshly ground)
1 cup Cranky's Tomato Paste
¼ oz. saffron
1 cup Parmesan cheese (freshly grated)
1 qt. white wine
2 cups Cranky's Sauce Rouille
3-4 loaves French bread

In all bouillabaisse recipes, saffron is a must and can be used to suit the individual tast and color of the broth. The amount can vary. If a rich flavor and color is desired, use more. Simple enough.

Clean and fillet all of the fish, saving the heads, skins and bones and place them in a large stock pot with sea salt, pepper, the studded onion and the 2 cups of vegetable mixture. Bring to a boil and simmer for 1-2 hours to make a rich fish stock from the fish in the recipe. While this is on simmer set the fillets in the refrigerator. After an hour or two … crush the heads and bones with a large ladle and cook as long as it takes to reduce the liquid by one third. Strain the stock through a fine sieve and set aside in a stainless steel bowl. In a large earthenware pot with high side walls, pour the olive oil, adding the onions, parsley, fennel, bay leaves and thyme when the olive oil begins to bubble. When the onions are translucent, add the tomatoes, garlic, tomato paste and orange rind and simmer until the tomato liquid has evaporated. Dissolve the saffron in the wine and pour this into the pot and stir. Bring to a slow boil, season with the salt and pepper, add the fish stock from the stainless steel bowl and simmer for 10-12 minutes. Cut the eel into 2 inch length pieces cut the firmer fish fillets in tbsp size pieces. Cut the John Dory and the cod into 8 fillets each. Turn the flame down very low, and with a flat strainer, put the langoustines in the bottom of the pot followed by all of the firm pieces of fish. Lastly, gently lay the fillets on the top. Cover the pot and turn up the flame to medium and cook for about 9-10 minutes. Remove from the stove and let stand for about 5 more minutes, still covered. Most people like to separate the pieces of fish and eel and lobster from the broth … I do not. I prefer to ladle the broth from the fish into large bowls and distribute the fish and lobster into each bowl. This way, the fish doesn't get as cold as quickly. I then rub the French bread on the outside with some garlic butter, cut in 2 inch slices and placed in a large bowl. I then drip olive oil on the bread and Parmesan cheese and pop in the oven for a minute or two. Serve everything in the center of the table and at once so that the fish does not get cold. Sprinkle the bouillabaisse with the rest of the Parmesan, parsley and Cranky's Sauce Rouille. (Serves 8-10)

Fins, Shells and Such

The bountiful wonders of Mother Nature's waterways could conceivably feed the peoples of the world without their ever planting one grain of rice, or raising, for market, one domestic farm animal. However, our balanced diet would be a little diminished. However, the existing balance is not only appreciated, but it makes dining much more enjoyable. The harvest that is taken from the world's waterways yearly is truly astounding but not inexhaustible. We, as consumers and individual of our pantries, must take great care that we do not deplete this marvelous and mysterious climate that Mother Nature provides and tends with great care with very little help from mankind.

In this section of this little cookbook, I have attempted to touch on as many points of interest and general information that will help to provide this much needed assistance to this marvelous keeper of the world's root cellar. I have included a list of one hundred bits of information that will help the reader understand how these waters have influenced the development of different cuisines throughout the world.

I have also added a list of tips for the cook as to the handling of the different seafood along with a buying guide to insure the freshest of product that will result in the proper moistness and gustatory delight while protecting the consumer from any illness that can result from the consumption of improper preparation and old or spoiled seafood.

I cannot suggest more strongly that this portion of Cranky's Cookbook and Kitchen Helper be read carefully and thoroughly. The results that you produce from the hearth will be worth the time.

Facts You Possibly Didn't Know about Seafood

Did you know that:

Mankind has captured and eaten fish almost as long as he was near water? That bone fishhooks were found in a cave in Norway dating back almost 5,000 years ago?

Mummified bodies of Nile perch have been found in the tombs of the pharaohs?

Mankind knows less about the 328 million cubic miles of water he calls the oceans and seas than he does about the other side of the moon?

Fish fossils have been found in ancient farm areas indicating that the land was at one time submerged?

Fish bones were found in the tillable land areas of ancient cultures, indicating that fish was probably eaten by the farmers or used as fertilizer for their crops?

Pliny used a shark's brain boiled in oil as a relief for a toothache/

The same mixture was used in the case of a bite from a rabid dog?

Explorers discovered that salted tuna flesh would ease viper bites?

Pliny also discovered that the blood, spleen and liver, that were called collectively, depilitory, would remove unwanted body hair?

Gesner claimed that the heart, the liver and the gall of the pike and pickerel would cure ague and lower fevers?

The ashes of a burnt pike or pickerel were used to dress old wounds?

The gonads of certain fish, mainly the testes of salmon, were considered aphrodisiacs, a role later replaced by the oyster when mankind finally learned to eat one?

The discovery of cod liver, which led to A & D Ointment, has hundreds of uses such as oiling the hands of fisherman to ward off the severe chapping of hands cause by the howling gales at sea and the exposure to salt water?

Cod liver oil was first ingested on the basis that if it cures one thing, it might cure another, and a remedy for rickets was miraculously found by some brave fisherman with no taste buds?

Fish and shellfish are the most perishable foods in our pantry?

Fish that are caught by the sportsman can and have spoiled in the basket creel, in the boat cooler and on the stringer, especially if the water in the fish tank gets warm or the stringer isn't completely submerged ... especially in the warm summer months?

The oil in the salmon causes discoloration of the rest of the beautiful pink or red flesh, if not chilled properly?

Five species of the pink Pacific Salmon will only discolor about 10 percent of the time, possible because of the salt content. This is unexplainable since these species have much higher oil content.

Mussels will open after steaming; if they do not open, they should be discarded?

Oysters should be tightly closed before steaming or served in any manner?

Clams should be tightly closed before steaming or served in any manner? If they close when they are poked with a knife, they are suitable for use. If there is no response, they should be discarded.

The Japanese started cultivating clams as early as 746 A.D. as far as we can discern, and it is believed that they started much earlier.

Soft shells clams or "piss clams" or steamers clams or long neck clams or Ipswitch clams should be discarded after soaking and cleaning if the necks do not retract, ever so slightly when flicked with the finger.

Mankind has blamed the poor little sea otter for destroying the abalone beds when, in reality, they were harvested by American fisherman in California and shipped to Japan and China where the shells sold for more that ten times the price of the meat where they were used for inlays for furniture, buttons and jewelry?

American Indians, such as the Seminoles and the Hurons, caught large mouth bass on lures made from deer hair back before the settlers arrived?

Bluefish, a sport's fisherman's delight in the Atlantic, at times have been witnesses chasing large schools of fish much larger that themselves through the water, biting off the tails and letting the rest float or get away?

Bluefish have also been seen disgorging themselves when they are full and then renewing the chase?

A Spotted Cow is the name of a salt water fish and a beer made in New Glarus, Wisconsin?

Fish killed suddenly by harpoon or hit on the head as soon as they are brought on board as opposed to being kept alive in a fish locker or on a stringer will be sweeter, fresher, less odiferous and tender?

Bouillabaisse has been mentioned in over 200 poems and songs, mostly written by the peoples of Marseilles, France in order to promote "their original dish." The reason that I say this is that over 100 of these poems and songs have been written by the friendly folk of Marseilles?

Carp was farmed raised in China over 1500 years before Christ and was transplanted to Europe as early as 350 B.C., according to Aristotle ... how the dickens Aristotle got to China in his lifetime ... if he truly existed ... is somewhat of a mystery. According to a five volume work written by Jan Dubravius entitled, "About the Fish Ponds and Fish Lining Therein", it is stated that over 450,000 acres of breeding ponds for carp and whitefish were a going business in Moravia and Bohemia around 1547, the year that his work was written?

Catfish have been caught as large as 600 pounds, with the largest on record being caught in Russia at 660 pounds?

A 660 pound catfish has a mouth large enough to swallow a full sized Holstein dairy cow weighing in excess of 2000 pounds?

When pressed with your finger, the flesh of fresh fish will be firm and elastic and your finger will not leave an indentation?

The eyes of fresh fish will not be cloudy or sunken ... they will be clear and not sunken and not milky?

The gills will be bright red and not ashen gray which indicates the length of time oxygen and blood have been absent from the gills?

Fresh fish will have an aroma that somewhat resembles sliced cucumbers?

Its characteristic skin color should be unblemished by any reddish patches or discoloration along the ventral area?

Fresh fish will taste sweet?

Fresh fish will never smell "fishy?"

Properly handled, frozen fish will never taste "fishy?"

You can normally tell if the fish being displayed in a fish market is fresh by the initial odor that greets you at the door?

A rancid odor in most oily fish, such as mackerel, salmon, cod, smelt, herring, and lake trout, is an indication of improper handling?

The real golden "golden caviar" that was served to the Czars of Russia doesn't come from a sturgeon? It is the roe of the starlet, a fish related to the sturgeon but almost extinct?

Clam shells served as wampum or money in the Eastern Colonies of America? The black wampum made from the dark purple of quahogs was more valuable than the white wampum made from conch shells?

According to the log of John Cabot, upon his return to England to report to his sponsor, Henry VII, the fish were so numerous off the coast of what we now call Newfoundland that all you had to do to catch a boatload was to lower weighted buckets into the water over the side of the ship?

In the 1600's, the Atlantic cod was the main success of the slave, molasses and sugar trade? This was due to the demand of the European market for salt cod. A ship would deliver a load of salt cod to Spain or Portugal, make a run to West Africa for slaves, trade the slaves in the West Indies for molasses and sugar, which would be purchased by the distilleries in New England in order to make their favorite liquor. This was called the "Golden Triangle" and was in full bloom well into the 1700's.

The largest "fish and chips" restaurant in England, Harry Ramsden's in Yorkshire, deep fries over 500,000 pounds of fish per year along with 1,000,000 pounds of potatoes?

Fish should be deep fried at temperatures between 350° and 390°?

When planking a fish for cooking, one should be careful not to use wood that was painted or stained at one time and never use wood that is highly resinous, such as pine? Use only hardwoods that are dried and well cured.

The coasts of North America are responsible for eighty percent of the crab population or edible crabs in the world?

The crayfish is the center of attention of breakfast in Scandinavia and Finland, the main ingredients in the "Louisiana Crawfish Boil," found on the battle shields of the Houma Indians, and that the ownership of the crayfish fishing grounds was the final clause in the peace treaty between the Maori people of New Zealand and Great Britain which gave the locals the title, so to speak?

The dolphin, or mahi-mahi, is a fish and should not be confused with the dolphin or porpoise, the mammal?

If you freeze your catch, it should be well wrapped with as little air as possible and, after the packages are frozen solid, they can be ice glazed by dipping in 35° water and refrozen? This will prolong freshness for two or three months longer.

That groupers mature as females in 3-4 years, the become males?

The herring industry was so important that in 1360, King Valdemar IV of Denmark tried to take over the Skane Fishery and ware lasted for two years? He was defeated by the Hanseatic League.

The English staved off the attack of the French at the battle of Rouvray for a short while by rolling out barrels of salted herring and using them as a barricade? This only prolonged the defeat by the French led by Joan of Arc in 1429 at Orléans. It was called the "Battle of the Herrings."

The Seven Year War between the Dutch and the English was over the possession of the cod fishing grounds off the Newfoundland banks?

Lobster was so plentiful in the 1600's in America and until the early 1800's that it was used for bait to catch large sea bass?

The spiny lobster of the Bahamas, before breeding season, migrate in single file along the bottom of the ocean to new grounds so that their young will have proper nourishment? It is called the "Crawfish March."

The meat of a lobster is the same texture no matter how old or how large they get to be?

Lobsters have been caught by trawlers off the coast of North America that weigh in exces of sixty-five pounds?

Main lobsters are either left-handed or right-handed? The crusher claw is larger whether on the right or left.

The French word for mackerel is maquereau, which means an oily person who makes his money off the services of ladies of the night.

The little threads that come out of a mussel are called byssus?

The byssus are formed by the mussels secreting a liquid that hardens when it hits the sea water?

The women of ancient Greece would collect these little threads and weave them into gloves that were worn by the fishermen? They had to be kept moistened or they would harden—they were stored in buckets of seawater and were handed down from generation to generation—a true test of their durability.

The Romans cultivated oysters over 2000 years ago? They transplanted oysters from the shores or Brundisium and put them in a region called Lucrino?

The Japanese cultivated oysters in the 1600's?

An oyster in a daily feeding will pump 25 gallons of water through its body in a twenty-four hour period?

The oyster is a vegetarian and derives its nourishment from small marine plants called diatoms?

The greenish colored flesh of the Marennes oysters in France are the most desirable to taste because of the high content of copper and iodine?

The name of the dish Paella Valenciana comes from the name of the pan in which it is prepared—a paelleras?

Pompano walk across the water on their tails and have been known to circle a boat in single file while the boat is traveling forward at high speed?

The bones of salmon have been found in the caves of Stone Age Man in Southern Europe and have been carbon-dated to the year 25,000 B.C.?

American Indians of the Columbia River Valley revered the salmon as a food and also gave it a high place in their religious ceremonies and their mythology?

There is no such fish as a sardine? Sardines are any of a hundred different fish with soft bones that belong to the herring family?

In Greek mythology, the goddess Aphrodite is said to have risen from the sea in a chariot made of scallop shells and drawn by six seahorses?

Coquilles St. Jacques is named after the apostle St. James who used the scallop shell as his personal emblem? The pilgrims to his shrine carried it like a badge?

The sea cucumber is an ocean slug and not a vegetable?
Shrimp grow up to 30 inches in length?

There are over 250 species of snapper in the world's seas?

Eighty percent of a squid is edible?

The coastline of the Chesapeake Bay is larger than the total coastline of the United States between Maine and the state of Washington?

The striped Bass was so plentiful when the pilgrims landed on the coast of Massachusetts that it was the main staple of the early diet before crops could be raised and was also the fertilizer for farmers?

The funding for the first public school in the New World was funded by the striped bass industry?

All sunfish or bluegill are edible?

The swordfish is not very afraid of ships or any floating objects, such as rafts and many a ship survivor has lost his raft to the swordfish?

Trout is the most universally farmed or cultured fish in the world, both for angling as well as for the table?

Dom Pichon, a monk in the sixteenth century, artificially impregnated trout?

All trout can be cooked the same and are delicious in any recipe that is designed for either trout or salmon?

Tuna, the beef of the sea, attain weights in excess of sixteen hundred pounds?

Tuna were commercially caught by the Phoenicians during the early days of Carthage about 600 B.C.?

The Walleye is a relative of the trout and salmon and along with its desirability for the tender and tasty white meat; it also supplies the world with a caviar substitute?

Happy Fishing! Happy Eating!!

A Buying Guide for Seafood

Whole Fish

The scales should be shiny, bright and metallic and tightly adhered
The eyes should be bright, clear and full with black pupils and transparent corneas
The odor should be fresh and seaweedy—never fishy
The fish should be completely clean and well-rinsed
The flesh should be firm and very elastic
If the gills are in, they should be bright red or pink (preferably they should be removed when cleaning)

Fresh Fillets

Seaweedy odor
Firm, elastic flesh and clear translucent color
Well cleaned, trimmed, boned and skinned
No bruising to the flesh, blood spots or browning

Smoked Fish

Bright, glossy appearance
No signs of mold, dried blood or salt crystals
Clean, smoke odor
Firm texture

Live Oysters, Clams and Mussels

Shells are hard and unbroken
The bottom shells of oysters should be deeply cuped

Shells of clams and mussels should be tightly closed or close quickly when touched
Soft shell clams should show some movement of the neck when touched

Live Lobsters, Crabs and Crayfish

They should be cold and sluggish but having movement
No cracks or breaks in the shells
The lobster or crayfish tails will curl under when picked up
The weight should seem heavier for the size

Fresh-Shucked Oysters

Liquor should be clear and opalescent—not cloudy or gritty
Meats should be plump and immersed in the liquor
Meat color should be creamy
No strong odors

Fresh or Thawed Scallops

Color should be creamy white or a pinkish tan
Strong, sweet briny odor should prevail
Firm and slightly translucent flesh

Fresh or Thawed Shrimp

Firm flesh completely filing shell
No blackened edges or black spots on shells
Shell and flesh should not be slippery
No strong odors

Fresh or Thawed Squid

Firm flesh
No tears in skin
Skin is cream colored with purple to reddish-brown spots
Yellowing and pinkish coloration are tell-tale signs of aging

Cooked Lobster, Crab or Shrimp

Bright red shells
Meat should be moist

No strong odors
Picked lobster meat is snowy white with red tints
Crab meat is white with red or brown tints
Shrimp meat is white with red or pink tints

Surimi Seafood

Moist and firm but not slippery
Meat is opaque with and off-white color
The meat's surface should have red or pink, shellfish-colored tints
No strong odors

Frozen Seafood

Solidly frozen with glossy surfaces
No signs of frost inside package
Flesh is evenly colored with no white patches (sign of freezer burn) or orange coloration (sign of spoilage)
Packaging is undamaged with no signs of thawing and refreezing
No strong odors

Seafood Handling Guide

Whole Dressed Fish

To avoid bruising large fish such as salmon, lift them carefully using both hands. Rinse under cold running water and place directly on ice. Store the fish in the refrigerator. You should use the same day for the best taste but use at least within one to two days.

Fillets and Steaks

Rinse in cold running water pat dry with a paper towel and place in re-sealable plastic bags. Nest bags in ice. Use within one to two days.

Smoked Seafood

Always handle smoked seafood as you would fresh seafood. Place in re-sealable plastic bag. Store in coldest part of refrigerator.

Live Lobster, Crab and Crayfish

Love lobster, crab and crayfish will remain alive for up to 24 hours. Place in plastic bag with small punctures to allow air circulation. DO NOT place directly on ice, in an airtight container or in water. Cook the same day they are purchased for best results.

Live Oysters, Clams and Mussels

Place in an open shallow container and keep moist by covering with clean damp cloth or paper towel. DO NOT place directly on ice, in an airtight container or in water. Use oysters within five days; clams or mussels within two days.

Fresh-Shucked Oysters

Store in original container fully submerged in their liquor. Place in coldest part of refrigerator. Use within five days.

Fresh or Thawed Scallops

Always store scallops in re-sealable plastic bag with their liquor and use within two days.

Fresh or Thawed Shrimp

Rinse in cold running water, drain and place in re-sealable plastic bag. Nest bag in ice and refrigerate. Use within two days.

Fresh or Thawed Squid

Clean and store in re-sealable plastic bag, refrigerate and use within one to two days.

Cooked Lobster, Crab or Shrimp

Place cooked whole crab or lobster in rigid re-sealable container. Use within two to three days. Place crab or lobster meat in re-sealable plastic bags. Use within three to four days. Store pasteurized crab meat in refrigerator for up to six months, unopened in original container.

Surimi Seafood

Store thawed in refrigerator in a re-sealable container for no more than 14 days.

Leftovers

Refrigerate leftover seafood within two hours of cooking. Cool quickly. Use within one to two days. Never longer!

Cranky's 100 Tips for the Cook

1- Don't grab the handle of an iron skillet with a damp rag while removing same from a hot oven.

2- Always have an Aloe Vera plant in your kitchen window next to your fresh herb plants in case of burns.

3- Too much oil in the pan can saturate anything you fry and also boil over and set your stove on fire.

4- Every kitchen or barbecue pit should have a small fire extinguisher within arm's reach.

5- When deep frying in "hot oil," make sure that items submersed are not saturated with water unless you are trying to start another fire.

6- Salt is like sand—it puts out fires and heals wounds.

7- An egg will lie on its side in a bowl of cold water if fresh. If the egg lies at an angle, it is about 3-4 days old and 7-10 days old if it stands on end.

8- Never heat bread, pastry, or any other flour product in the microwave unless you enjoy dining on rubber.

9- Wet your knife between each cut when slicing hard boiled eggs.

10-If you have egg yolks that are left over after cooking, put them in a cup with some salad oil. The yolks will remain soft and can be used later in many different recipes.

11-A drop or two of vinegar in the water will prevent eggs from cracking when hard boiling.

12-Salt in the water will do the same thing.

13-The juice from a baked apple pie can be easily removed from the oven floor if salt is poured on it. This will help to burn the juice to a crisp and make it easier to remove.

14-Rubbing fresh lemon juice on your hands is useful for removing fish odor from your hands. This will be useful in cleaning utensils and your cutting board.

15-Lemon juice can also do the same for onion or garlic odors.

16-Dip your bananas in lemon juice to prevent browning. The lemon juice also adds a delightful flavor.

17-While baking bread, a small dish of water in the oven will help keep the crust from getting hard.

18-For better results, always preheat your cookie sheets, muffin tins or cake pans.

19-Rinse your bowl with boiling water when you are creaming butter and sugar. They cream faster.

20-When melting chocolate in a sauce pan, grease the pan lightly to prevent burning.

21-Potatoes soaked in salt water for 20 minutes will bake more rapidly.

22-Poke the potatoes with a fork and they will not explode in your oven.

23-Rinse potatoes in cold water for an hour and they will fry crisper.

24-Muffin tins are great to bake stuffed peppers.

25-Sweet potatoes will not turn dark if soaked in salt water after peeling; neither will regular potatoes.

26-To crisp the skins of baked potatoes, brush lightly with bacon grease 10-15 minutes before removing from the oven.

27-When boiling potatoes, add lemon juice to the water to prevent darkening.

28-To keep baked potato skins soft, wrap in aluminum foil.

29-Milk added to boiling water will make cauliflower whiter.

30-A little cup of vinegar on the stove will cut down the odor of cabbage, broccoli, or asparagus while cooking.

31-If you heat a lemon in hot water and roll it on the cutting board, it will yield more juice.

32-Soak an orange in boiling water before peeling and the white membrane will come off with the skin.

33-Sometimes whipping cream takes a long time to whip. If so, add 2-3 drops lemon juice or a bit of gelatin power to it and it will whip to the desired sized peaks.

34-Pie crust will turn out lighter and better if all the ingredients are cold.

35-Poke holes in the bottom crust so the air doesn't push it out of shape during cooking.

36-Fold the top crust over the lower crust before you crimp the edge and the pie will leak less during baking.

37-A teaspoon of vinegar will make a flakier crust for pies.

38-Too much liquid makes pie crust tough.

39-Milk instead of water makes a softer and flakier crust.

40-A small amount of baking power lightens a pie crust.

41-To gloss the top of a pie crust, brush with a mixture of 1 egg, 1 teaspoon sugar, ½ teaspoon salt, and 1 teaspoon vegetable oil just before baking.

42-Vanilla adds flavor to any fruit pies.

43-Always bake a custard pie at high temperature at first to prevent a soggy under crust.

44-If you knead the mixture for about a minute after mixing, it will generally improve the texture of baking powder biscuits.

45-Cool cake halves before frosting.

46-A cake is done when it shrinks from the sides of the pan and springs back in the center when touched lightly with a finger.

47-Asparagus stalks should be green, not white, and the tips closed. Use the same day because asparagus toughens rapidly.

48-Beans with small seeds and no wrinkles are fresher.

49-Choose berries with few stems. They might be under-ripe.

50-Flowered vegetables like broccoli, cauliflower and Brussels sprouts, should be tightly closed and not discolored.

51-Cabbage and lettuce should be chosen by weight and color. Heavy heads are normally not infested with bugs and worms and are less likely to have black rot.

52-Cucumbers should be long and slender and dark green. These will have smaller seeds.

53-Peas and lima beans should have well filled pods but not bulging.

54-Very large root vegetables such as parsnips, turnips, beets, carrots and radishes might tend to be woody.

55-Citrus fruit should be chosen that are heavy for their size and avoid fruits that have soft, withered, or sunken areas.

56-Cantaloupes are ripe when the netting in the skin design is yellow and the end opposite the stem is soft to finger pressure.

57-Honeydews are ripe when the color is yellowish. Pretty green ones are not ripe.

58-Watermelons must have a yellow color on one side. IF they are white or pale green on one side, they are not ripe.

59-Nuts will come out of the shell in halves if soaked overnight in salt water before cracking.

60-Popcorn should be frozen to keep it fresh—you will have fewer un-popped kernels.

61-If you sprinkle popcorn lightly with warm water and let stand a few hours before popping, it will pop better.

62-Rub cheese that is to be stored for a while with some butter or olive oil and it will not harden.

63-Any egg slicer can be used to slice beets and mushrooms as well as eggs.

64-A pinch of baking soda added to icing will keep it from cracking.

65-A pinch of baking soda whisked into a sauce, soup or gravy that has separated will bring the mixture back together.

66-A lemon half dipped in salt will clean copper pots.

67-A slice of raw potato will take ballpoint pen ink off vinyl, sometimes!

68-Hard boiled eggs soaked in beet pickle juice make for an interesting taste treat and colorful garnish.

69-Marshmallows can be cut very easily if you butter or oil your scissors.

70-Chilled marshmallows will not stick as much.

71-Salt should be added to lettuce by the diner. Salt tends to wilt or toughen lettuce.

72-Well tossed salads use less dressing and are crisper than those that are served dry and have had salad dressing poured over them.

73-Never store carrots with their tops; the tops will drain the roots of their nutrients and flavor.

74-Ingredients for salads, after dicing, chopping, shredding or slicing, should be lightly rinsed with cold water, strained and placed in an airtight Ziploc bag. This will keep them fresh and very crisp.

75-Oil a salad mold lightly. The aspic or gelatin salad will slip out easier.

76-All shellfish meat in the lobster and shrimp families toughens when cooked too long.

77-Do not test broiling meats with a fork. The juices will run out. Use your finger and learn the different textures of Blood Rare, Very Rare, Rare, Medium Rare, Medium, Medium Well and Well.

78-Steaming clams and oysters too long makes them tough and dry.

79-Layered fish should be served as soon as the flesh flakes but is still moist. Dry fish is a sin.

80-Fish and seafood are more susceptible to marinades and seasoning than meat and the times and amounts should be adjusted accordingly.

81-Clams, mussels and oysters should be scrubbed well so that the broth derived is clearer, cleaner and more flavorful.

82-Crabmeat is the sweetest of all shellfish and the seasonings are interchangeable recipes (i.e. lobster or crab quiche) have to be adjusted slightly.

83-All seafood can be marinated or pickled and served à la ceviche.

84-Fish stock will be more flavorful if the fatty tissues of certain fish are left out of the pot.

85-Adding a small amount of vinegar to a court bouillon will make the fatty tissue in fresh water fish such as salmon and lake trout become firmer and easier to remove.

86-Rub the outside of steaks with a small amount of oil and seasoning when grilling, and the marking will be more clearly defined.

87-Marbling in steaks should never be confused with lines of gristle. A finger nail scraped on a white line will come up short of fat when gristle is encountered.

88-Meat does not have to be U.S. Prime or U.S. Choice to be good; however, it must be aged properly.

89-Beef should be aged for at least two weeks; four is better but Cranky prefers 6-8 weeks.

90-Aged meat shrinks and the coloring gets darker.

91-Pork can be cooked on the pink side if you know your butcher.

92-Game birds and dry white meat fowl, like turkeys and capons, should be cooked on the breast or drumsticks down so that the moisture remains in the breast and the oils from the rest of the bird flow toward the breast. This is especially true with turkey, capons, pheasant and running birds.

93-When using a needle to inject liquors or liquids into roasts, try to get the needle next to the bone or center of the roast. If you just inject the liquids into the center of the flesh, you will be boiling or steaming the meat and defeating the purpose.

94-When you are buying any type of wild game birds or wild game animals; try to find out the diet and age. This can be determined by knowing the area of origin. The older the game animals or game birds; the drier the meat will be and the tougher it will be. Larding might be necessary.

95-When shish-kebobbing, always spear the meat against the grain. There is less chance of loss and drying.

96-Lamb should be cooked on the pink side to preserve the maximum flavor.

97-Lamb or mutton cooks faster that most meats, giving he fat or fatty tissue an unpleasant consistency. Therefore, a roast should be kept hot while carving, and all cuts or chops should be served on "hot" platters.

98-Veal should always be served rare and moist.

99-Milk fed veal is always pink.

100-When cooking on a spit, the animal should always be secured and positioned so that the animal is upside down just after the back has passed the fire. This preserves the juices. Also the fire should only be on one side of the animal.

Cranky's Grilled Salmon with Hollandaise

8-1 inch salmon steaks (boned and with the skin removed)
½ cup olive oil
2 tbsp. lemon rind (grated)
1 tsp. sea salt
2 tsp. thyme (freshly chopped)
1 cup dry wine
4 tbsp. shallot (minced)
2 tbsp. cold water
2 cups Cranky's Hollandaise Sauce
2 lemons (wedged)

In a shallow dish, combine the olive oil, the lemon rind, the salt and the thyme. Put the salmon steaks in the marinade dish. Turn them to coat with the marinade. Cover the dish and refrigerate for 2 hours, turning about three or four times. Transfer the salmon with a slotted spoon to the broiler that has been turned on and is hot already. Brush with the marinade and broil on each side for 3-4 minutes at the most. Transfer the salmon to a heated serving dish, serving the salmon smothered with the Hollandaise sauce. (Serves 8)

Cranky's Barbequed Broiled Salmon

10-12 pound salmon (without head)
1 cup butter
1 cup parsley (freshly chopped)
2 cups Cranky's BBQ Sauce
3 lemons (wedged)
1 tsp. sea salt
1 tsp. black pepper (freshly ground)

Split the salmon and remove all of the bones. Place the salmon sides in a hinged fish broiler, with the skins together. Brush the salmon flesh with olive oil and salt. Mix the butter, parsley, lemon juice and the BBQ sauce together and brush the flesh of the fish. Broil the salmon, flesh side down for about 2-3 minutes or a light golden brown. Nearly all fish can be cooked this way and are absolutely delicious. (Serves 8)

Cranky's Salmon in Strawberry Pepper Wine Sauce

2 cups red wine
2 pounds strawberries (hulled and sliced)
4 tbsp. parsley (freshly chopped)
2 tbsp. butter
1 tbsp black peppercorns (crushed)
½ tsp sea salt
1-8 oz. salmon fillets (boned and skinned)
1-2 ozs. lemon juice
½ cup wine
2 lemons (wedged)

Place the fillets in a shallow roasting pan. Pour the lemon juice and white wine on top and cook at 450 degrees in your oven until cooked through but still moist. In the meantime, bring the red wine to a simmer adding the parsley, butter, salt and peppercorns to the pan. Add the strawberries and cook until they still hold their shape but are cooked through. Transfer the salmon to heated plates and smother each serving with the strawberry pepper wine sauce. (Serves 8)

Cranky's Salmon with Cucumber and Tomato Sauce

8-6 oz. salmon fillets
4-5 large cucumbers (peeled, seeded and julienned)
1 cup butter
3-4 cups Cranky's Fish Stock
5-6 tbsp shallots (minced)
2-3 cups heavy cream
¼ Cranky's Tomato Paste
3 tbsp butter (softened and cut into pieces)
½ tsp. sea salt
½ tsp black pepper (freshly ground)
1 cup white wine
2 tbsp chives (freshly snipped)

In a saucepan, blanch the cucumbers in lightly salted water for 1 minute and drain them quickly. Sauté the cucumbers until tender in some butter and set them aside. In a saucepan, combine the fish stock and the shallots and reduce the stock to a glaze. Add the heavy cream, whisk the mixture briskly and reduce the mixture by one half. Add the tomato paste and the cucumbers, along with the softened butter and stir gently. Set aside and keep the sauce warm. In a buttered oven-proof skillet, place the salmon fillets that you have lightly sprinkled with salt and pepper. Add the wine. Poach the fillets in the wine for 3-5 minutes in a 325 degree oven. Transfer the sauce to a heated serving dish, arrange the salmon fillets on top and garnish with the rest of the softened butter and the freshly snipped chives. (Serves 8)

Cranky's Poached Salmon

½ cup Cranky's Sorrel Butter Chiffonade
3-4 pounds salmon fillets (skin removed and boned)
½ tsp. sea salt
½ tsp. black pepper (freshly ground)
2-3 cups dry vermouth
1 cup heavy cream
3 egg yolks (lightly beaten)

Slice the fillets into one half inch strips and lay them on a baking sheet large enough to accommodate the whole batch in one layer. Sprinkle with the salt and the pepper. Pour in the dry vermouth over the fish. Cover the fish with wax paper that has been buttered. Bake at 350 degrees for 5 minutes. Transfer the salmon with slotted spatula to a heated serving dish, and keep it warm. Reduce the cooking liquid over high heat, adding any juices that accumulated in the serving dish, for 2 minutes. In a small bowl, whisk the cream into lightly beaten egg yolks. Reduce the heat under the juices and whisk in the egg mixture, heat to a simmer. Whisk in the Sorrel Butter Chiffonade and add the salt and pepper to taste. Blanket the salmon with the sauce. (Serves 8)

Cranky's Salmon Steaks Teriyaki Style

8-8 oz. salmon steaks (skinned)
3-4 cups Cranky's Teriyaki Sauce and Marinade
8 cups cooked rice

Marinate the salmon steaks in the marinade for 40-50 minutes, turning them once half way through the time period. Turn on the broiler and broil the steaks in the marinade for about 6 minutes without turning. Transfer the steaks to heated places with a ring of rice. Spoon the remaining juices over the salmon and serve at once. (Serves 8)

Cranky's Salmon Soufflé

4 tbsp. sweet butter
2 tbsp. Parmesan cheese (grated)
2 tbsp. shallots (minced)
¼ cup flour
1½ cups hot milk
2 tsp. Cranky's Tomato Paste
2 tsp. mustard
1 tbsp. lemon juice
4 large egg yolks
½ cup sharp Cheddar cheese
1 ½ to 2 cups cooked, flaked salmon (about 1 pound before cooking)
1 tbsp. sea salt
Tabasco sauce
1 tbsp. parsley (freshly chopped)
7 large egg whites (whipped)
½ tsp. cream of tartar

Put a baking sheet on the rack in the lower third of the oven and set the oven at 400 degrees. Butter a 2 quart soufflé dish with butter. Sprinkle the bottom and sides with the Parmesan cheese and refrigerator the dish. Melt the remaining butter in a saucepan over low heat. Add the shallots and sauté lightly. Whisk in the flour and cook slowly for about 2-3 minutes, stirring constantly. Gradually whisk in the hot milk, ¼ cup at a time, mixing until smooth. Bring the mixture to a slow boil and whisk in the tomato paste, mustard and the lemon juice. Simmer for 3 minutes. Put the egg yolks in a small bowl, add about a quarter of the hot liquid and whisk briskly until smooth. Add this mixture to the saucepan. Bring the mixture back to a slow boil, stirring, and simmer for 1 minute. Remove the pan from the heat and blend in the Cheddar cheese, mixing until very smooth. Fold in the salmon. salt, Tabasco, and the parsley. Make sure that the soufflé base is well seasoned before adding the egg whites and the crème of tartar. Empty the mixture into the soufflé dish. To form the "top hat" of the soufflé, insert a spatula into the batter one inch from the edge. Move the spatula up and down as you turn the dish, so that you have made a complete ring around the edge of the dish. Put the soufflé in the oven on the heated baking sheet. (This helps to bake the bottom) and reduce the oven temperature to 375 degrees. Bake the soufflé until golden brown for 35-40 minutes. The top of the soufflé should wobble slightly. Serve immediately. (Serves 8)

Cranky's Codfish with Chipotle Butter and Black Beans in Papillote

4 plum tomatoes
8-8 oz. cod fillets
36 green olives (pitted and halved)
1 red onion
1 cup white wine
4-6 tbsp. lime juice (freshly squeezed)
8 sprigs of oregano
8 pieces of string
1-16 inch squares of parchment
1 recipe Cranky's Chipotle Butter
1 recipe Cranky's Marinated Black Beans

Place the green olives and red onion in the food processor and chop coarsely. Place a piece of parchment on a work surface and put about 3 tablespoons of the beans in the center with 2-3 slices of the tomatoes on top. Top this with a fillet of cod. Put 2 tablespoons of the olive and onion mixture, two tablespoons of white wine, 2 teaspoons of lime juice, 1 sprig of oregano a one tablespoon of the chipotle butter on top of the fillets. Tie the parchment together with the string. Repeat this process eight times. Bake the sacks for 15-20 minutes in a 400 degree oven … the cod should be cooked but moist. Serve the little paper sacks on hot platters and let your guests cut the paper away. (Serves 8)

Cranky's Salmon with Saffron Cream Cheese

3 cups dry white wine
1 cup shallots (minced)

2 cups heavy cream
1 oz. dry sherry
Saffron (generous pinch)
2 tbsp. olive oil
8-8 oz. salmon fillets
Sea salt to taste
Black pepper to taste (freshly ground)

Boil the wine and the shallots in a heavy saucepan until the liquid is reduced to about 4-6 tablespoons. Soak the saffron in the dry sherry. Add the cream and the sherry and the saffron, simmer until the total is reduced to 1 ½ cups, stirring constantly. This takes about 10-15 minutes on medium heat. Strain into a bowl, pressing as much of the solids through the strainer. Season the liquid with the salt and pepper to taste. Heat some oil in a very large skillet. Season the salmon fillets with some salt and pepper. Sauté the salmon fillets, about 3-4 minutes on each side. Transfer the fillets to hot platters. Smother the fillets with the sauce. (Serves 8)

Cranky's Salmon with Tequila and Tomato Vinaigrette

8-6 oz. salmon fillets
6 tbsp. mild chili powder
12 tbsp. olive oil
2 cups Cranky's Tequila and Vinaigrette

Make a mixture of the olive oil and chili powder. Rub the fillets with the mixture and sear on both sides for about 3-4 minutes a side or until cooked but still moist. Place the salmon fillets on heated platters and spoon the Tequila and Tomato Vinaigrette over the salmon fillets. (Serves 8)

Cranky's Stuffed Rainbow Trout

8 Rainbow trout (10-12 ounces each)
Cranky's Rainbow Trout Stuffing
1 cup port
1 cup Cranky's Fish Stock
1 carrot (chopped)

2 tsp. thyme (freshly chopped)
1 cup heavy cream
2-2 tsp. Cranky's Golden Roux
½ cup butter (melted)
3 tbsp. flour
3 tbsp. parsley (freshly chopped)
3 lemons (wedged)
Sea salt to taste
Black pepper to taste (freshly ground)

Stuff the cavities of the trout with the stuffing and sew up with some string. Choose a large enough pan or casserole dish to accommodate eight whole trout and cover with the port, carrots, thyme and the fish stock. Place the pan in a 325 degree oven and bake for 25-30 minutes. Transfer the fish to heated platters. Strain cooking liquid into a saucepan and whisk into the cream. Thicken the sauce with the golden roux. Salt and pepper to your taste. Add the lemon juice and the remaining port. Whisk until smooth and pour the sauce over the fish and serve at once. Garnish with the lemon wedges and parsley. (Serves 8)

Cranky's Halibut Steaks with Pistachio Crust and Wild Mushroom Sauce

1 cup Cranky's Pistachio Crust/Breading
2 cups Cranky's Wild Mushroom Sauce
8 halibut steaks

Shake the halibut steaks in the pistachio crust/breading and bake the fish at 350 degrees for no longer than 9-11 minutes. Serve the steaks on heated platters, smothered with the mushroom sauce. (Serves 8)

Cranky's Blackened Cajun Fish

Do not try this in your kitchen unless you have a ventilation hood over your stove. It just might smoke you out of your house. However, it works real well outside on an open fire or you BBQ grill. I have found that an open wood fire works just great, but a charcoal fire is just no hot enough. The skillet used in this method of cooking must get hot past the smoking stage ... the closer to white ash forming on the skillet bottom, the netter. Any one of the following fish can be used to make this wonderful Cajun dish and you will not be disappointed … redfish, salmon, red snapper, orange roughy, pompano, tilefish, stripped bass or bluefish.

8 fillets of the fish of choice (fresh and 8-10 ounces)
1 ½ tsp. onion powder
1 ½ tsp. garlic powder
1 ½ tsp. cayenne pepper
1 tsp. white pepper (freshly ground)
1 tsp. black pepper (freshly ground)
2 tsp. thyme (freshly chopped)
2 tsp. oregano (freshly ground)
1 pound butter (lightly salted and melted in a large skillet

Heat a large iron skillet (upside down) on the top of the stove until almost white hot and the smoke has disappeared. Do not forget that this has been done. Do not grab the handle. This will be far from a pleasurable experience. Mix all of the ingredients together and pour on a serving platter and sprinkle each fillet with the seasoning. Place on the hot skillet and pout a tsp of melted butter on the fish. Be careful … it might flame up. Cook until the underside is slightly charred, turn and repeat the process. Serve the fillets, piping hot on heated platters. Add all of the remaining seasonings to the melted butter and serve a small portion with each fillet in an individual ramekin. (Serves 8)

Cranky's Swordfish Casserole

8 swordfish fillets (6-8 ounces each)
¼ cup olive oil
Sea salt to taste
Black pepper to taste (freshly ground)
1 large onion (diced)
1 sweet green pepper (seeded and chopped)
6-8 medium tomatoes (peeled, seeded and chopped)
½ pound mushrooms of choice (sliced)
2-4 cloves garlic (Minced)
1 cup white wine
Cranky's Bouquet Garni I
2 lemons (juiced)

2-3 cups Cranky's Fish Stock
2-3 tbsp. flour
3-4 tbsp. butter
2-3 tbsp. capers
3-4 tbsp. pimientos (chopped)

Heat the olive oil in a large casserole and lightly brown the steaks on both sides. Salt and pepper the steaks and add the onions, green pepper, tomatoes, mushrooms and the garlic to the casserole. Simmer for ten minutes. Add the white wine, bouquet garni, the lemon juice and the fish stock. Cover the casserole and bake for approximately 30-35 minutes at 325 degrees. Transfer the steaks to heated platters and reduce the liquid to half, discarding the bouquet garni. Make a roux with the butter and flour and thicken the sauce. When the sauce is the proper thickness and very smooth, add the capers and the pimientos and smother the steaks with the sauce and serve piping hot. (Serves 8)

Cranky's Pompano é la Toulouse Lautrec

Toulouse Lautrec was not only a famous artist of the Impressionistic Period, he was also considered by his contemporaries to be an accomplished chef and would often cook for large groups of people at Monet's estate in Giverney, France outside of Paris. Here is his recipe, unchanged and taken from the English translation of his notes by Maurice Joyant when he published Lautrec's recipes in a cookbook from the master's very own notes.

4-1 ½ pompano (fresh if possible)
½ tsp. sea salt
Pinch of white pepper (freshly ground)
3 large onions (chopped)
1 pound unsalted butter
1-2 cup flour
5-6 cloves garlic (minced)
2 sweet green pepper (minced)
4 ounces capers
1-2 tsp. Tabasco Sauce
¼ cup Worcestershire Sauce
6-7 green onions (minced)
1 cup pimientos

2 tbsp chervil (freshly chopped)
½ cup parsley (freshly chopped)
2-3 lemons (wedged)
10-12 large mushrooms (sautéed)

Fillet the whole pompano and set aside. Place the bones, skin and heads in a large kettle with 4-5 quarts of water, some of the onion, salt and pepper and simmer for about 3-4 hours. Crush the heads of the fish and simmer for 2 more hours until the fish stock is reduced to 2 cups. Strain and set it aside. Melt ½ pound butter in a large cast iron skillet. Add the remaining onions, green pepper and the garlic and sauté for about 5-6 minutes. Stir in the capers, fish stock, Tabasco sauce, Worcestershire sauce, sea salt and a pinch of white pepper. Stir well. In a separate large skillet mix the flour and the butter together and cook slowly until a light brown color is achieved. Stirring constantly, add the fish stock mixture and stir until it is smooth. Add the green onions and simmer for about 5-6 minutes. Salt and pepper the fillets and dust with the flour. Bake the fillets on a cookie sheet in a 450 degree oven for 7-10 minutes or until the flesh is flaky but moist. Do not overcook! In the meantime, sauté the sliced mushrooms and set them aside until the fish fillets are ready to serve. Carefully place the fillets on hot platters. Stir the pimientos and the chervil into the sauce and pour over the pompano. Garnish with the lemon wedges and the chopped parsley and surround with sautéed mushroom slices. (Serves 8)

Cranky's Halibut with Wild Mushrooms

8 pieces of halibut
¼ cup butter (melted)
Paprika
1 pound wild mushrooms (sliced ¾ inch thick)
4 tbsp. tarragon (freshly chopped)
8 ozs. whole leeks (coarsely chopped)
4 ozs. butter
3-4 cloves garlic (minced)
¾ cup bourbon
2 cups Cranky's Chicken Stock
1cup cream
1 tbsp. sea salt

1 tsp. white pepper (freshly ground)

Place the halibut portions on a cookie sheet and brush them with the melted butter. Dust with the paprika and set aside. Combine the mushrooms, tarragon, leeks, garlic and butter in a sauté pan. Add the bourbon and flame the mixture. Stir in the chicken stock and the cream. Bring the mixture to a simmer and cook for 5 minutes. Add the salt and pepper to season. After it cools, place the mixture in a food processor and pulse to leave the mixture on the chunky side. Place the halibut in the oven at 375 degrees and cook until just underdone ... flaky and very moist. Ladle the sauce over the fillets, return to the oven and cook for about 2-3 minutes longer. (Serves 8)

Cranky's Turbot with Green Peppercorns

4 pounds of turbot fillets
½ cup shallots (minced)
1½ cups water
1½ cups white wine
2 tbsp. Cranky's Tomato Paste
4-5 tsp. arrowroot
½ cup heavy cream
4 tbsp. green peppercorns
Sea salt as needed
Black pepper as needed (freshly ground)
Paprika as needed

Sprinkle the fillets with some salt and place them in a flat casserole dish along with the shallots. Cover with the wine and the water. Poach the fillets until the flesh flakes. Transfer the fillets to a serving platter with a slotted spoon and keep warm. Strain the liquid and reduce to about 3 cups. Whisk in the Tomato paste and the arrowroot that has been dissolved in some cold water and simmer, stirring often until thickened. Add the heavy cream and the green peppercorns and simmer of a few minutes until the proper consistency is reached. Nap the fillets with the sauce, sprinkle with paprika and serve at once. (Serves 8)

Cranky's Baked Mahimahi

4 pounds mahimahi fillets
1 cup lemon juice
½ tsp. sea salt
½ tsp. black pepper (freshly ground)
2 tbsp. peanut oil
8-10 slices of bacon
1 tsp. tarragon (freshly chopped)
2 cloves garlic (minced)
½ pound butter (melted)
4 tbsp. parsley (freshly chopped)
2 limes (wedged)

Marinate the fillets in the lemon juice for 20-30 minutes. In the meantime, cook the bacon until crisp and set aside. Add the peanut oil to the bacon fat along with the tarragon and the garlic. Remove the fillets from the lemon juice and pat dry. Sprinkle with the salt and pepper and sauté in the peanut oil and bacon drippings. When the fillets are cooked but still moist, remove to heated platters, pour the melted butter over them and garnish with the chopped parsley and lime wedges. (Serves 8)

Cranky's Baked Whole Red Snapper

8 pound whole red snapper
½ tsp. sea salt
½ tsp. black pepper (freshly ground)
½ tsp. paprika
1 tbsp. Worcestershire sauce
1 tbsp. lemon juice (freshly squeezed)
½ cup better (melted)
2 cups white wine (dry) ¼ cup almonds (slivered)
3 cups Cranky's Brussels Sprouts Gratinée
3 cups Cranky's Glazed Carrots
3 cups Cranky's Cauliflower Gratinée
¼ cup parsley (freshly chopped)
2 lemons (wedged)

Scale the snapper and remove the gills. Rub the inside with a mixture of salt, pepper, Worcestershire sauce and the lemon juice. Place the fish on its side, head to the left, dorsal fin away from you. Pour the butter over the fish and add the wine and the almonds into the pan. Place the fish in the oven at 450 degrees and cook until the flesh is moist and flaky. Baste frequently to prevent drying. Serve on a large platter surrounded by the Brussels sprouts, carrots and cauliflower. Pour the pan dripping over the fish and serve at once, garnished with lemon wedges and chopped parsley. (Serves 8)

Cranky's Saucy Snapper with Bay Shrimp

4 tbsp. olive oil
2 celery stalks (finely chopped)
1 medium onion (finely chopped)
½ sweet green pepper (seeded and chopped)
1 tsp. fennel seeds
¼ tsp. dried crushed red pepper
2 cups crushed tomatoes
¼ cup dry white wine
2 tbsp. Cranky's Tomato Paste
8-8 ounce red snapper fillets
1 cup flour
½ pound cooked bay shrimp
Sea salt to taste
Black pepper to taste (freshly ground)

Heat the olive oil in heavy large saucepan over medium heat. Add celery, onion, green pepper, garlic, fennel seeds and the crushed red pepper and sauté until the vegetables are soft but not browned. Mix in the crushed tomatoes, wine and the tomato paste. Simmer the mixture until it thickens. Season the fillets with the salt and pepper. Coat them with the flour. Sauté the snapper fillets about 2 minutes per side. Simmer until fish is just cooked through. Remove the fillets to warm plates. Add the bay shrimp to the sauce and pour over the fillets. (Serves 8)

Cranky's Picasso Stripped Bass with Truffles

4 quarts Cranky's White Wine Court Bouillon for Fish

1-5 pound striped bass (heads off, fins and tail removed and scaled, bone in)
4 cups Cranky's Red Mayonnaise
3 tbsp. Cranky's Tomato Paste
6 hard boiled eggs (whites and yellows separated)
6 tbsp. Cranky's Fines Herbes
4 black truffles (fresh chopped)

Mix the tomato paste with the court bouillon and simmer for 30 minutes and then cool. Tie the bass in cheesecloth, leaving long ends for the easy removal of the fish from the poaching broth. Place the fish in the poacher and pouch for 20 minutes. Remove from the heat and let the fish cool in the pouching liquid. After it is cool, place the fish on a large serving platter. Remove the cheesecloth and the skin completely with great care. Dry the bass and pat it with a paper towel. Coat the fish smoothly with half of the red mayonnaise; put the rest into a pastry bag with a small serrated tip. Make your own patterns with the red mayonnaise on the bass. Garnish with the egg whites and the egg yolks, the fines herbes and the truffles that have been sliced very thinly. Pass the remaining red mayonnaise in a separate serving dish. Strain the poaching bouillon and save for future use … this can be frozen. (Serves 8)

Cranky's Poached Sea Bass with Seaweed

4 pounds whole sea bass
1 quart dry white wine
1 tsp. sea salt
½ tsp black pepper (freshly ground)
4 pounds seaweed (to pack lobsters, available at the fish market)
1 Recipe Cranky's Sauce Pistou

Sprinkle the bass fillets with the salt and pepper. Place the fish in a poacher and pour the wine over the fish. Spread the seaweed over the fillets. Add enough water to cover the fillets. Poach for about 20 minutes or until the fish flakes when tested with a fork. Remove the seaweed and transfer the fillets to heated plates and serve with Cranky's Sauce Pistou. (Serves 8)

Striped Bass with Flaming Fennel and Pernod

10 pound striped bass (head and tail removed, scaled and skin on)

30 some fennel twigs
½ tsp. sea salt
½ tsp. black pepper (freshly ground)
1½ pound butter
1 cup shallots (chopped)
2 pounds mushrooms of choice (sliced)
4 cups Cranky's Fish Stock
4 cups white wine
2-3 ozs. Pernod
2-3 cups Cranky's Sauce Gregoire
4 cups Cranky's Parsley Potatoes

Season the inside cavity with the salt and pepper and 7-8 fennel twigs and score the bass 6-8 times on the top side, inserting a fennel twig in each slit. Dot the bottom of a large fish cooker or deep baking pan with some of the butter and spread the shallots and the mushrooms on the bottom. Carefully place the bass on top of the vegetables and pour in enough wine and fish stock to cover half of the fish. Add a dash of Pernod and bake the fish for 5 minutes at 450 degrees. Reduce the heat to 350 degrees and bake for about 30 minutes more. Baste the fish at least 4 times during the cooking. With the remaining fennel twigs, make a bed on a large serving platter. Carefully the bass from the cooker and place it on the bed of fennel twigs. Sprinkle the twigs with some Pernod. Heat the rest of the Pernod in a ladle, ignite and pour over the pre-soaked fennel twigs and let them extinguish themselves. Serve the bass on hot dinner plates with parsley potatoes and Sauce Gregoire. (Serves 8)

Cranky's Poached Sea Bass with Sweet Peppers

4-2 pound whole striped bass (heads removed and scaled)
Sea salt to taste
Black pepper (freshly ground)
1 sweet green pepper (seeded and minced)
1 sweet red pepper (seeded and minced)
3 tbsp. shallots (minced)
2 tbsp. chives (freshly snipped)
2 cups dry white wine
1 cup dry vermouth
1 cup Cranky's Fish Stock

1 cup butter (softened)
4 cups cooked rice
Tomato slices as needed
Lemon slices as needed

Sprinkle the bass cavities with the salt and pepper. In a large buttered roasting pan, arrange the fish on top of the mixture of the salt, pepper, vegetables and chives on top. Place the tomato and lemon slices on top of the fish and add the wine and the vermouth and the fish stock and bring the liquid to a boil. Place the pan in a 450 degree oven and cook for 10 minutes. Baste and cook for 20 minutes or until the flesh of the bass is flaky. Transfer the fish to a large heated platter with a slotted spoon and keep warm. Garnish this with some more lemon and tomato slices. Strain the cooking liquid into a sauce pan and scatter the vegetables on top of he cooked fish. Reduce the liquid by half and remove the pan from the heat. Add the butter, 2 tablespoons at a time and season with salt and pepper to taste. Top the bass with the sauce and serve with the cooked rice, placed on heated platters in a ring. (Serves 8)

Cranky's Sea Bass with Mushroom Stuffing

8-10 ounce fillets striped bass
3 cups Cranky's Fish Stock
1 cup butter (melted)
3 cups stale bread crumbs
2 cups dry white wine
1 egg (lightly beaten)
3 cups Cranky's Duxelles
1 hard boiled egg yolk (sieved)
2 tbsp. parsley (freshly chopped)
2 tbsp. chervil (freshly chopped)
2 tbsp. chives (freshly snipped)
½ tsp. sea salt
¼ tsp. black pepper (freshly ground)
1 tbsp. shallots (minced)
¼ tsp. thyme (freshly chopped)
2 cloves garlic (minced)
2 small bay leaves (crumbled)
1 stick of butter (softened)

In a bowl, blend the butter and the bread crumbs. Add the wine, beaten egg, Duxelles, egg yolk, parsley, chives, chervil, sea salt and black pepper. Combine them well. Place each fillet in a buttered gratin dish. Sprinkle the bass fillets with the shallots, thyme, garlic and bay leaf. Salt and pepper the fillets to taste. Cover the fillets with the stuffing. Pour the wine and fish stock in the dishes but do not submerge the stuffing. Cook the fish in the dishes at 350 degrees for about 10-12 minutes or until the flesh is flaky. Pour the liquid from each dish in a saucepan and reduce to one third the volume. Swirl in the butter in small chunks until the sauce is smooth. Place the sauce in a heated sauceboat and serve with the fillets, after they have been placed under the broiler until the stuffing is a golden brown. (Serves 8)

Cranky's Sole Marguery

8-10 ounce sole fillets
24 mussels (scrubbed and bearded)
2 cups dry white wine
8 shallots or 2 small onions (finely chopped)
½ tsp. sea salt
½ tsp. black pepper (freshly ground)
6-8 tbsp. butter
6-8 tbsp. flour
24 shrimp (small to medium size, cooked and peeled and deveined)
4 egg yolks
1 cup heavy cream
2 cups Cranky's Fish Stock

Steam the mussels until they all open and remove from the shells. Discard the unopened mussels. Put aside. Strain the mussel liquid, add the shallots and the wine and simmer for about 5 minutes. Place the sole fillets in the broth and poach for about 3-4 minutes or until just starting to flake. Remove to heated platters with a slotted spoon. Melt 4 tablespoons full of butter and make a golden roux with the flour. Add the fish stock and thicken with the roux. Simmer on a very low heat for about 4-5 minutes or until the flour is cooked. Add the mussels and the shrimp. Beat the egg yolks into the heavy cream. Quickly whisk this mixture into the sauce pan and thicken but do not boil. Swirl in the remaining butter and smother the fillets with the mixture. (Serves 8)

Cranky's Sole Duglere

Try to skin the Dover sole when it is ice cold or partially frozen. Make a cut on both sides of the sole just behind the gills at the top of the head. Take a dry cloth and pull the skin from the head to the tail. Cut off the heads and gut the fish. I like to throw all of the heads and the skins in a freezer bag and freeze, in order to make fish stock at a later time.

8 fillets of sole
10-12 tbsp. butter
4 shallots (minced)
4 medium tomatoes (peeled, seeded and diced)
2 tbsp. parsley (freshly chopped)
½ tsp. thyme (freshly chopped)
1 small bay leaf (crushed)
½ cup dry white wine
1 cup Cranky's Fish Stock
Sea salt to taste
black pepper to taste (freshly ground)
1 cup light cream
½ cup Cranky's Golden Roux
2 lemons (wedged)

Remove the heads of the sole, gut the fish and then skin the whole fish as explained above in italics. Melt some butter in a large skillet that has a cover. Arrange the fillets in the pan and smother with the fish stock, wine, shallots, tomatoes, parsley, thyme, bay leaf salt and the pepper. Dot the fillets with five or six pats of butter. Cover and simmer for about 10 minutes or until the fish flakes. Remove the fillets to a heated platter with a slotted spoon and keep warm. Reduce the broth by one half. Thicken the broth with the roux, and when it is smooth, simmer on a very low flame until the flour is properly cooked. Whisk in the cream and simmer for 1-2 minutes more. Remove from the heat and stir in the remaining butter. Pour the sauce over the fish and serve with the lemon wedges on the side. (Serves 8)

Cranky's Sautéed Dover Dole

8-1 pound Dover sole

½ cup butter
2-3 cups Cranky's Sauce
2 lemons (wedged)
Paprika
Flour

Prepare the sole as in the previous recipe and lightly dust with the flour and sauté the fish in a large skillet. While the sole is cooking, warm the sauce and pour a 2-3 ounce ladle full in the middle of the warmed serving plates. Separate the cooked fillets from the bones and gently place them on the sauce. Sprinkle with a small amount of paprika and garnish with lemon wedges. Serve this dish immediately (Serves 8)

Crank's Braised Dover Sole

8-1 pound Dover sole
1-1 ½ cups red wine
1-2 tsp. anchovy paste
1 cup butter
2 tsp. parsley (freshly chopped)
2 lemons (sliced)

Prepare the sole as in the previous recipe. Melt the butter in a cookie sheet and lay the filleted fish on the butter. Blend the anchovy paste and the red wine together and pour this mixture over the fillets. Cover the sheet with aluminum foil and bake for about 8-10 minutes in a 400 degree oven. Serve the sole on heated platters, pouring the wine, butter and anchovy mixture over the fish. Garnish with the parsley and the thin slices of lemon. (Serves 8)

Crank's Sole with Cucumbers and Caviar

8 sole fillets
4 cucumbers (peeled, halved, seeded and cut julienne style)
½ tsp. sea salt
½ tsp. black pepper (freshly ground)
2 tbsp. butter
3 cups Cranky's Fish Stock
½ cup Cranky's Crème Fraîche

4 tsp. Sevruga or Beluga caviar

Sauté the cucumber slices along with the nutmeg, the salt and the pepper in butter for about 2 minutes, or until they are translucent, but still crisp. Drain and set aside on some paper towels. In a heavy saucepan, reduce the fish stock to 2 cups, whisk in the crème fraîche and simmer until smooth and thickened. Add one half of the caviar, remove from the heat and keep warm. Fold the sole fillets in half and put them in the top of a steamer. Steam until they are opaque. Reheat the cucumbers and make 8 small mounds on a heated serving platter. Place the steamed fillets on the top of these cucumber piles with a slotted spoon. Add the rest of the caviar to the sauce and smother the sole filets and serve at once. (Serves 8)

Cranky's Sole Normande

16 mussels (scrubbed and bearded)
8-10 large button mushrooms (stems removed and peeled)
2 tbsp. shallots (chopped)
2 cups dry white wine
½ tsp sea salt
1 tsp. black pepper (freshly ground)
8 sole fillets
8 oysters (freshly shucked)
2 cups Cranky's Velouté Sauce
3 tbsp. butter
2 tsp. lemon juice (freshly squeezed)
4 egg yolks (beaten)
16 cooked shrimp (shelled and deveined)
2 dashes Tabasco Sauce

Put the mushroom peelings and the stems, chopped finely, into a pan along with the shallots and the wine. Add the mussels and steam them until they are all open. Remove the mussels from the shells and set aside. Discard the unopened mussels, remove the mussels from the other shells and reserve the broth. Salt and pepper the fish, Fold the fillets, lengthwise, and place them in a lightly buttered pan with a cover. Add the strained mussel broth and the remaining broth and simmer for about 5-6 minutes, covered. Add the oysters and simmer until the oysters start to curl. Place the fillets on heated platters with a slotted spoon and set the broth back on the heat, minus the oysters and reduce to about half. Add this quickly to hot velouté sauce and simmer on very low, stirring constantly. Meanwhile, poach the mushrooms caps for 6-8 minutes in a little warm water with some butter, salt and lemon juice. Add this liquid to the sauce and reserve the mushroom caps. Pour a little of the hot sauce into the beaten egg yolks, beating constantly, and fold the sauce into the saucepan. Add the mussels, shrimps and Tabasco sauce to correct the seasonings, heat and stir but do not boil. Smother the fillets with the sauce. Place an oyster on each fillet and top each fillet with a mushroom cap. (Serves 8)

Cranky's Sole Normande Riche

Add 2-3 tablespoons of Cranky's Lobster Butter à la Maison to the finished sauce and garnish with a thin slice of black truffle.

Cranky's Basted Seafood Skewers

1 quart Cranky's Fish and Fowl Marinade
3 pounds halibut fillet (cut into 2 inch cubes)
24 shrimp (peeled and deveined,)
4-5 sweet green or red or yellow or a combination thereof (seeded and cleaned and cut into 1" squares)
6 small onions
8 long skewers.

Marinate the fish, shrimp, onions and peppers in a glass bowl for about 45 minutes. Divide the items evenly on the skewers. Cook slowly over medium hot-charcoal or gas fired barbeque, turn and baste frequently with the marinade. Cook about 15-20 minutes or until the halibut and shrimp are done to a turn. (Serves 8)

Cranky's Fish Fillets with Shrimp Sauce

8-8 ounce whitefish fillets
½ tsp. sea salt
½ tsp. white pepper (freshly ground)
½ cup white wine
¼ pound butter (cut into pieces)
4-6 ounces cooked "titi" shrimp

2 tsp. parsley (freshly chopped)

Season the fillets with the salt and pepper and place them on a cookie sheet. Pour the wine over the fillets and dot the fillets with the butter. Bake until the fish is opaque and transfer to a heated platter or heated plates. Pour the pan juices into a saucepan and reduce to about three quarters of a cup. Add the shrimp and the parsley and simmer until desired serving temperature. Taste the sauce and adjust the seasoning with some salt and pepper and whatever you desire and spoon over the fillets. (Serves 8)

Cranky's Barbequed Skate

3-4 tbsp. olive oil
4-5 pounds of skate wings (skinned)
1 quart Cranky's Sensational BBQ Sauce
4 lemons (wedged)

Cut the skate wings into 8 equal portions. Start your BBQ and oil the grill with some olive oil when the coals are right. Brush the wings on both sides with a liberal amount of the BBQ sauce. Place the wings on the grill and allow them to cook for 3-4 minutes, dousing the flames as necessary. Turn the wings, brush with some more BBQ sauce and cook until the skate wings are opaque … about 4 minutes longer. Serve with heated sides of BBQ sauce on the side and some lemon wedges. (Serves 8)

Cranky's Otak-Otak

18 banana leaves
¼ cup coconut (freshly grated)
1 tsp. hot peppers (crushed)
4 cloves garlic (minced)
½ tsp. tumeric
1 tsp. curry powder
½ tsp sea salt
1 cup Cranky's Coconut Cream
3 pounds swordfish, halibut or red snapper
48 small cooked "titi" shrimp (shelled, peeled and deveined)

If some banana leaves are available, blanch them first in boiling water. Sometimes, young palm fronds can be substituted for the banana leaves, as a last resort. Spread the leaves after draining and prepare to stuff them. Bake the coconut on a cookie sheet at 400 degrees until it is golden brown. Process the toasted coconut, along with the tumeric, salt, peppers and the garlic. Add the coconut cream and mix thoroughly and place in the top of a double boiler; cook the mixture until it is thick. Cut the fish into thick slices. Mix the shrimp and the coconut cream mixture together. Spread half of the shrimp on the leaves in the center part of the leaves. Arrange the fish slices on top of the shrimp mixture and then top the slices with the rest of the shrimp mixture. Fold the leaves as to make a little package and secure the leaves with toothpicks. Bake them for 20 minutes at 425 degrees or roast them slowly over a charcoal fire. (Serves 8)

Whole Live Maine Lobster

This delicacy of the depths has been boiled, steamed, broiled, fried, baked, stewed, casseroled, quiched, sautéed, pickled, stuffed, ceviched, curried, souffléed, bisqued, moussed, croqueted, newburged and thermidored. Heck, the Germans even make strudels with the little critters.

In short, the Maine lobster tastes wonderful regardless of the dish and which ever way it is prepared. The difficulty, it seems, is in the first stages of preparation where the problems arise.

Toulouse Lautrec told his friends at Monet's country house that the best way to cook an old hen or rooster was to chase it down the road with a shotgun loaded with fine bird shot and when it appears to be scared out of its wits, shoot it. The muscles will tense up just before death and be tender when relaxed.

I am not recommending killing lobsters with firearms but I do recommend sudden and violent death. The lobster, like the shrimp and scampi, if cooked too slowly or too long, will become tough and rubbery and lose all of the natural sweetness and flavor. In the event that a lobster is placed in cold water and lulled to sleep from a sense of kindness and anti-cruelty thoughts, you will find that the flesh of a boiled lobster, especially the meat derived from the tail section, will tend to be quite rubbery and not as sweet as usual. By plunging the lobster into boiling water, you cause an immediate tensing of the muscles, and, soon after, a relaxation leaving the cooked flesh tender, tasty, and sweet.

This is automatically accomplished whenever you split a lobster for broiling. After all, it is quite a shock to any living creature to be split in two and have various herbs and spices thrown into the open wounds. However, the bet way to cook a lobster and retain all of its natural juices, flavor, and sweetness and still end up with tender morsels is to steam the creature.

All of the lobster recipes in "Susie's Cookbook and Kitchen Helper" are for the preparation of a 1-1/2 pound "female" live Maine lobster. This is what I consider to be a full size portion. If I wish to use any of the lobster recipes to make a hot or cold appetizer, I normally use a 1 pound "female" live Maine lobster and cut the recipe by one third. Whenever possible, I try to use the seaweed that comes with the lobsters for boiling or covering the lobsters when steaming.

Following are some of my most favorite ways to prepare Main lobsters, and I hope you try each and every one. Get cracking!!!

Some Personal Lobster Hunting Experiences

Years ago, while attending Rhode Island State College, prior to their changing the name to the University of Rhode Island and just before electricity, I hired on as a not-so-able hand or steersman on a lobster boat. I can't remember the name of its captain ... as a matter of fact; I don't think I ever knew him by anything other than skipper.

However, I did manage to learn a good deal about the sea and a smattering of the lobsterman's trade ... the most important of which being that if you were not capitalized to the degree of a complete start-up ... stay out of the business. I learned very quickly how Mother Nature could quickly and efficiently put you out of business with a five minute storm.

I read an article about the lobster trade not very long ago and it mentioned that as of 1993, between 55 and 60 million pounds were Canadian. I didn't know how we managed to squeeze the Canadians out of the industry and only hope that they get some small share of the pie.

Since reading that article I have been informed that the 50-60 million pounds mentioned was actually the true amount of lobsters landed by the American fisherman in U.S. waters only and an additional 100 million pounds was harvested yearly by the Canadians. I was also informed by a gentleman at CALPA (Canadian Atlantic Lobster Promotion Association) that the fines levied on fisherman that violate these very stringent but invisible territorial guidelines are extremely stiff indeed.

How the mystique of the "Maine" lobster came about is somewhat of a mystery since the early settlers of the Massachusetts Bay Colony were some of the first Europeans to tear apart a freshly caught and boiled lobster. The size and abundance of the catch was well documented so why not call them Massachusetts lobster? If we study further we will find that the Pilgrims ceased eating lobsters as soon as they could hunt or raise their own food ... definitely preferring to consume creatures of a more desirable appearance and less plentiful. It is human nature to desire the rare and expensive, relegating the plentiful or common to the poor. I read somewhere that lobsters were so plentiful in the seventeenth, eighteenth, and nineteenth century that only the poor would eat them. At one point, it is mentioned that the colonists even crushed the lobsters and used them as fertilizer in their fields. What the hell, don't the poor always get the sh ... ty end of the stick.

One story, true or not, relates that John D. Rockefeller was the reason for the lowly lobster to jump from the poor men's stew pot onto the dining tables of the well-to-do. As the tale unfolds, John D. established a summer home on Mt. Desert Island off the coast of Maine. It is said that a bowl of lobster stew intended for the servants table was mistakenly sent upstairs where it was devoured with great gusto. John D. gave it a permanent spot on his menu not only on the island but back in New York where the rest of the rich and famous ... the famous 400 ... embraced this ugly little creature like a long lost relative ... as long as it was made with Maine lobsters and nothing other than Maine lobsters.

As a result, the simple but delicious fare of the poor became the darling of the rich and simply too expensive for the average peoples of the world to have on their dinner table. What's New???

Cranky's Chilled Live Maine Lobster with Majestic Cocktail Sauce

Lobsters have no central nervous system and therefore have no sense of pain to hot or cold temperatures. They are cold blooded animals. In Toulouse Lautrec's cookbook, there is a recipe for a range chicken ... it states ..."chase the chicken down the street and kill it suddenly with a small pellet shotgun ... as to not to destroy the flesh ... this will terrify the chicken and causing the muscles to tense ... much like "rigor mortis." When cooked the flesh will then relax and be tender when the warming of the cooking process returns the flesh to a normal state." Therefore, not only is it not correct that lobsters have feelings ... it is also correct that the crueler that you get with them ... the better and more tender the meat.

1-1½ pound live Maine lobster (female preferred)
½ cup Cranky's Majestic Cocktail Sauce
5-6 sprigs of dill
2 tsp. parsley (freshly chopped)
¼ tsp. sea salt
1 tsp. lemon juice (freshly squeezed)
1 tsp. paprika
1 tbsp. Cranky's Classic Mayonnaise
1 lemon (wedged)
1 head of Boston lettuce

Bring a large kettle to a rolling boil and then turn to a simmer. Add the dill, parsley, salt, pepper, lemon juice and paprika. **PLUNGE** the live lobsters into the boiling water and cook until the white lobster butter starts to float to the top. Skim this off and save. Remove the kettle from the heat and let set for 20-30 minutes. A good rule of thumb in the boiling of lobsters is eight minutes for the first pound and one minute for each additional pound. At any rate, when finished cooking and setting off of the heat for about 10-15 minutes, remove the lobsters from the water and let them drain. After they are drained, chill them in the refrigerator. Save the liquid in mason jars and add a handful of fresh dill to each quart. Freeze this liquid every time that you steam or boil a lobster.*1 Using a chef's knife, remove the legs from the body and freeze to make lobster stock in the future. Split the lobster down the middle lengthwise. Throw away the gall bladder sac in the head and the intestinal tract in the tail section. Chill Well! Carefully take the liver (tomalley) and the coral (roe) out of the head and body of the lobster along with all of the white lobster butter. Add this to the lobster butter that you skimmed from the pot and process it in a food processor along with the mayonnaise and the paprika. Spread this on the tail meat of the lobster and then fill the body cavity wit the cocktail sauce. Crack the front claws and serve one claw and a wedge or two of lemon. (Serve one whole lobster as a dinner or lunch or one half of a lobster as an appetizer.)*2

1-I use the same lobster water or lobster stock for future boiling or steaming. Whether it is my imagination or not, the lobster seems to taste a great deal better when steamed over or boiled in the herb water.

2-This recipe can be served hot. Just warm the sauce for dipping. Treat the lobster as it were to be served right from the pot.

Cranky's Steamed Live Maine Lobster with Shellfish Butter

1-1 ½ pound live Maine lobster (female)
2-4 quarts Frozen Herb Water from your freezer *3
2-3 ozs. Cranky's Lobster Butter à la Maison (heated)
or
2-3 ozs. Cranky's Majestic Cocktail Sauce (chilled)

Place the lobster in the top of a steamer and the herb water in the bottom and cook for as long as you would when you boil a lobster ... start counting after the steam starts coming out of the steamer. Split the lobster down the middle lengthwise. Throw away the gall bladder sac in the head and the intestinal tract in the tail section. The lobster than can be served hot or cold. Serve one whole lobster per person, as an entrée or one half of a lobster as an appetizer. If you serve cold, use the cocktail sauce and lemon wedges. If hot, use the lobster butter and lemon wedges. (Serves 1)

3-I use the same lobster water or lobster stock for future boiling or steaming. Whether it is my imagination or not, the lobster seems to taste a great deal better when steamed over or boiled in the herb water.

Cranky's Broiled Live Maine Lobster with Parsley Butter

1 ½ pound live Maine lobster (female)
2 ozs. Cranky's Lobster Butter à la Maison
3-4 tbsp. Cranky's Parsley Butter
1 lemon (wedged)

Be sure that the lobster is alive and wiggly. Split the lobster from head to tail with a chef's knife and remove the intestinal tract in the tail section and the gall bladder sac in the head and discard. Place the halves on a cookie sheet along with the cracked claws and liberally butter the flesh and the claws with the lobster butter and broil for about 7-8 minutes or until the tail meat can be easily removed from the shell. Serve at once on a heated platter along with the melted parsley butter and lemon wedges.

Cranky's Charcoal BBQ Broiled Live Whole Maine Lobster

8-1 ½ pound Maine lobsters (female)
2 cups Cranky's Sensational BBQ Sauce
1 cup butter
2-3 lemons (wedged)

Split the lobster from head to tail with a chef's knife and remove the intestinal tract in the tail section and the gall bladder sac in the head and discard. Crack the claws; brush the lobster with the butter and broil, flesh down on a one eight inch wire screen. After 3-5 minutes, turn right side up, brush one more time and cover the BBQ. Let smoke for 2 minutes more. Remove to heated plates and serve with melted butter and lemon wedges. (Serves 8)

Cranky's Singapore Lobster Curry

1 cup butter
4 cups onion (finely chopped)
4 cloves garlic (minced)
½ tsp. cumin (powdered)
2 tsp. cinnamon (ground

1 tsp. allspice (freshly ground)
¼ tsp. cloves (ground)
½ tsp. nutmeg (freshly ground)
½ tsp. cayenne pepper (ground)
4 tbsp. curry powder
6 cups Cranky's Coconut Cream
4 small cucumbers (peeled, seeded and cubed)
4 whole live Maine lobsters (1-2 pounds each and female if possible)
10-12 slices of fresh ginger root
3 cups Cranky's Chicken Stock
4 tbsp. lime juice
1 tsp. sea salt
8-12 bowls of hot steamed rice

Melt the butter and sauté the onion and the garlic until soft but not burnt or brown. Add the cumin, cinnamon, allspice, cloves, nutmeg, pepper, curry and the coconut cream. Stir and simmer for 8-10 minutes on very low heat. Blanch the cucumbers, drain and add to the sauce. Remove the lobster meat from the claws and the tails and cut into bite sized pieces. Put the lobster meat and the ginger root to the sauce. Add the chicken stock and simmer for about 10 minutes on very low heat. Add the lime juice and the salt to taste. Serve on a ring of cooked rice. (Serves 8-12)

Cranky's Lobster Armoricaine

This recipe is not an "American" dish. On the contrary! While traveling in France through Brittany, a province on the northwestern coast of France, I came across a great many recipes that had the word Armorica attached to them. We owe this to the Gauls who were the first inhabitants of this rocky, but beautiful peninsula. They named it Armor, meaning literally, "the country by the sea." It was later inhabited by the Romans and finally pillaged by the Vikings for almost 300 years. In the sixth or seventh century, the Celts took over and evangelized the country and renamed it Brittany. However, down to the centuries, the old name sort of stuck and has been part of their cooking world ever since. Armoricaine, nowadays, is the name given to a very choice type of oysters that are found off the coast of Brittany. Some cookbook authors, however, have confused this very old and venerable name with "à l'Americaine." This recipe is not to be confused with "Lobster à l'Americain.," This recipe and name of a group of recipes, definitely owes its ances-

try to provençal. Although similar, they are very different in the final analysis and worth the tasting. So are the oysters ... they are delicious.

8-1 ½ pound live Maine lobsters (females)
1 cup olive oil
4 tbsp. butter
1 large onion (finely chopped)
3-4 cloves garlic (minced)
10-12 medium ripe tomatoes (peeled, seeded and diced)
1 cup Cranky's Tomato Paste
½ cup parsley (freshly chopped)
1 quart dry white wine
4 cups Cranky's Fish Stock
1 cup Cognac
¼ cup Pernod
1 tsp sea salt
1 tsp. black pepper (freshly ground)
½ tsp. cayenne pepper
2 bay leaves (crushed)
3-4 loaves of French bread
½ cup olive oil
½ cup Parmesan cheese (freshly grated)
½ cup parsley (freshly chopped)

Split the lobsters from the head to the tail. Remove the air sac in the head and the intestinal tract in the tail. Remove the tomalley and the roe or coral and reserve for the sauce. Crack the claws, cut the tails in small sections or medallions with a sharp knife, trying not to shatter the shells. Sauté the lobster pieces in the olive oil until the shells turn red and remove them to a separate platter immediately. Add half of the butter, onions and garlic and sauté for about 2 minutes. Add the tomatoes and the tomato paste, parsley, wine and the fish stock. Simmer this mixture for about 30-40 minutes or until the liquid has reduced to half the volume. Re-place the lobster pieces in the kettle and flame with the Cognac, allowing it to extinguish itself. Add the tomalley and the coral, the Pernod, salt, black pepper, cayenne pepper and the bay leaves. Stir in the remaining butter and serve in heated bowls along with the slices of French bread that has been sprinkled with olive oil, parsley and the grated cheese that has been warmed in the oven. (Serves 8)

Cranky's Lobster Tails with Black Beans

8-12 ounce lobster tails
2 cups black beans
1 cup olive oil
1 cup onions (chopped)
1 cup celery (chopped)
1 cup carrots (chopped)
4 cloves garlic (minced)
8-10 strips of bacon (chopped)
½ tsp. sea salt
½ tsp. black pepper (freshly ground)
20-24 pearl onions (cooked)
2 large tomatoes (peeled, seeded and chopped)
4 cups Cranky's Saffron Rice

Soak the beans in cold water for one hour. Rinse and boil until they are al dente. Cut the lobster tails lengthwise and lay the flesh on the top of the shells. Place them on a broiling pan and season with the salt, pepper and the garlic that you have soaked in the olive oil for 2-3 hours. Set aside. Sauté the beans with the onions, the carrots, the celery and the bacon pieces, until the bacon is semi-crisp. Add the tomatoes and the pearl onions and simmer until the tomatoes are cooked. Broil the lobster tails. Remove the flesh from the shells and serve them on top of the bean mixture that you have placed in a large heated platter. Ring the heated platter with the saffron rice. (Serves 8)

Cranky's Lobster l'Americaine

8-1 ½ pound whole live Maine lobsters
1 cup olive oil
4 celery stalks with the leaves intact (finely chopped)
3-4 carrots (scraped and finely chopped)
1 large onion (finely chopped)
2 tsp. thyme (freshly chopped)
5-6 garlic cloves (minced
1 tsp. black pepper (freshly ground)
4-5 bay leaves (finely crushed
4-5 tomatoes (peeled, seeded and chopped)

1 pint Chablis
2 cups Cranky's Tomato Purée
1 ½ quarts Cranky's Fish Stock
2 tbsp. green onions (finely chopped)
6 ozs. Cognac
½ pound butter
½ tsp. cayenne pepper (freshly crushed)
1 tsp sea salt
1 tsp. black pepper (freshly ground)
¼ cup parsley (freshly chopped)
¼ cup Cranky's Golden Roux
2-3 lemons (wedged)

Tear the lobster tails from the heads and separate the large claws from the head part. Set these aside after you have split the tails and cracked all of the claws. Cut the legs from the bodies and crush them with a meat mallet. Split the heads and save all of the tomalley and the coral in a small glass bowl in the refrigerator. Crack and chop the body and head and place all of these broken pieces into a large iron soup kettle. Add the olive oil, celery, carrots, onions, thyme, garlic salt and pepper and sauté for about 5-6 minutes on high heat ... stirring continuously. Add the bay leaves, chopped tomatoes, tomato purée, fish stock and the Chablis. Cover the kettle and simmer the mixture for about 40 minutes. Remove from the heat and strain the sauce through a fine piece of cheesecloth. Discard all of the solids. Return the liquid to the kettle and reduce to about one and a half quarts. Take a very large deep skillet and sauté the lobster pieces in their shells in the remaining olive oil. When the pieces start to turn pink, add the green onions, butter, salt, pepper, cayenne pepper and the Cognac. Flame the Cognac until it extinguishes itself. In the meantime, swirl the tomalley and the coral, from the refrigerator, into the broth in the kettle until it is blended together. Pour this over the lobster pieces I the skillet, cover and simmer for about 10-12 minutes or until the lobster pieces are bright red. Remove the lobster pieces to a large heated serving platter. Thicken the sauce with the roux and pour over the cooked lobster pieces. Garnish with the chopped parsley and lemon wedges, (Serves 8)

Cranky's Lobster Thermidor

8-1 ½ whole live Maine lobsters

1 cup butter
2 tbsp dill (freshly chopped)
½ cup shallots (chopped)
2 cups Cranky's Clam Broth
1 tsp. tarragon (freshly chopped)
1 tsp. parsley (freshly chopped)
1 tsp. chervil (freshly chopped)
4 cups Béchamel Sauce
2 tsp. dry mustard
2 cups Cranky's Beef Stock I
1 cup Parmesan cheese (freshly grated)
½ tsp. sea salt
1 tsp. black pepper (freshly ground)

Split the lobsters, taking out the intestinal tract and the air sac in the front of the head, reserving the coral and the tomalley. Brush the flesh of the lobsters and sprinkle with the dill. Bake for 10 minutes at 325 degrees ... do not overcook or burn the shells. Remove the meat from the claws and the tails, discard the claw shells or save in the freezer to make a future lobster stock. Remove the meat from the tails and the lobster butter from the heads ... you can cut off the legs and add these to the freezer package for later stock for lobster bisque. In a large saucepan put the remaining butter, shallots, white wine, clam broth, tarragon, parsley, and chervil. Reduce to half volume. Add the Béchamel sauce, the dry mustard, the beef stock, the tomalley and the coral. Bring to a boil and simmer for 5 minutes. Correct the seasoning with the salt and pepper and then force everything through a fine sieve. Arrange the lobster halves on a large baking sheet. Divide half of the sauce into the lobster shells, arrange the pieces of lobster on top of the sauce, cover the pieces of lobster with the remaining sauce and sprinkle with the grated cheese. Place in a very hot oven at 450 degrees for 5 minutes or until the tops are golden brown. (Serves 8)

Cranky's Lobster Bonnefoy

This is a delicious way to prepare live Maine lobster and not as difficult as it might seem. The most important part in cooking this recipe, as well as all shellfish, is the timing. Shellfish has a tendency to get tough and flavorless if overcooked.

8-1 ½ pound live Maine lobsters
1 pound butter
2 cloves garlic (minced)
15-20 whole black peppercorns
1 tsp. sea salt
2 cups Cranky's Tomato Purée
1 Cranky's Bouquet Garni III
3-4 quarts Cranky's Beef Stock I
1 quart white wine
½ cup parsley (freshly chopped)
5-6 large ripe tomatoes (peeled, seeded and chopped)
3-4 loaves of French bread
2¼ tbsp. olive oil
1 cup Parmesan cheese (freshly grated)
2 tbsp. parsley (freshly chopped)
3-4 lemons (wedged)

In a large soup pot, sauté the garlic in one fourth of the butter, and after properly cooked, add the fish stock, tomato purée, salt, peppercorns and the bouquet garni into the pot. Bring the mixture to a simmer. While this is happening, split the lobsters in half at the head and leave the tails intact. Remove the air sacs in the heads and the intestinal canals in the tails. Save the liquid, tomalley and the coral. Chop the tail sections in one half inch rounds and crack the claws and legs. Turn your attention back to the simmering liquid, adding the tomatoes, beef stock, white wine and the liquid from the split lobster, along with the tomalley and the coral to the pot. Let this simmer for about 40-45 minutes. Add the parsley and one half pound of butter. Let it cook or simmer for about 15 minutes over low heat, stirring often. Turn up the heat and reduce the sauce to about one half or about 2 quarts. In a large iron skillet, sauté the lobster rings in the remaining butter for about 8-10 minutes to harden the flesh slightly. Remove the pieces of lobster from the skillet and place them in a large earthenware container. Strain the sauce through a sieve, removing the bouquet garni. Most of the sauce should go through a sieve. Pour this over the lobster rings and place in a 325 degree oven for about 10 minutes or until bubbling hot. Serve with grated cheese sprinkled on the French bread that has been cut into circles and dipped into the olive oil. Serve with some lemon wedges. (Serves 8)

Cranky's Fricassée Lobster

1 cup carrots (finely chopped)
1 cup celery (finely chopped)
1 cup onions (finely chopped)
¼ cup dill (freshly chopped)
4 cups white wine
8 live Main lobsters (1 pound each)
4 tbsp. Cognac
2 cups white wine
1 cup heavy cream
¼ pound butter (melted)
½ cup sliced zucchini
½ cup baby carrots (peeled)
10-20 dill sprigs

Place the carrots, celery, onions, dill and the wine in a large kettle and bring to the boil. Add the lobsters and cover. Simmer for about 10 minutes. Remove the lobsters and split the tails. Remove the shells from the tail meat and set aside. Simmer the wine and the vegetables and reduce by half. Remove the meat from the claws and also set aside. Remove the coral and the tomalley and set aside. Chop the lobster body, claw shells and small legs and add to the pot along with the Cognac and simmer for 8-10 minutes adding the rest of the wine. Strain, return to the pot and reduce to half of the volume. Add the heavy cream and thicken. Whisk in the butter, the lobster meat that you have cut into bite size pieces, along with the coral and the tomalley. Remove from the heat and keep warm. Strain the zucchini and the carrots. Place the lobster heads on the plates and ladle the sauce and the lobster meat behind the empty lobster heads. Sprinkle the zucchini and carrots over the top and decorate the dish with the dill sprigs. (Serves 8)

Cranky's White Lobster Chili

2 cups onions (chopped)
5 garlic cloves (minced)
2 tbsp. vegetable oil
2 jalapeño peppers (seeded and chopped)
1-4 oz. can of mild green chilies (chopped)

2 tsp. cumin (ground)
2 tbsp. lemon juice (freshly squeezed)
1 tsp. oregano (freshly chopped)
½ tsp. cayenne pepper (ground)
½ tsp sea salt
2 cups Cranky's Chicken Stock
1 large can of white kidney beans (drained and rinsed)
1½ pounds of lobster meat (freshly cooked or canned and cut into bite size pieces)
½ cup fresh cilantro (coarsely chopped)
½ cup each of Monterey Jack cheese, Cheddar cheese, mozzarella cheese
½ cup Cranky's Salsa Rosa
2 tbsp. crushed red pepper flakes

In a large skillet, sauté the onions and garlic in the vegetable oil until the onions are translucent. Add the jalapeño peppers, chilies, lemon juice, cumin, oregano, cayenne pepper and the salt and cook for one minute. Add the chicken stock and the beans and bring the mixture to a boil. Reduce the heat and simmer uncovered until slightly thickened. Just prior to serving, add the lobster meat and gently bring to the proper heat. Stir in the cilantro. To serve, ladle into chili bowls and garnish with the cheese, some of the chopped cilantro, the red pepper flakes and the salsa rosa. (Serves 8)

Cranky's Broiled Maine Lobster with Parmesan Cheese

8 small live Maine Lobsters
2-3 tbsp. olive oil
6 tbsp. green onions (freshly chopped)
1 cup dry white wine
2 tsp. mustard (dry)
4 cups Cranky's Mornay Sauce
8 tsp. Parmesan cheese (freshly grated)

Split the lobsters, remove the head sacs and the intestinal tracks, and set the halves aside. Put the olive oil in a skillet and sauté the green onions. When they are soft, add the white wine and the dry mustard. Stir well and add the mornay sauce. At the same time, broil the lobster halves for about 2-4 minutes and remove from the broiler. Take the meat out of the claws and mix the meat with the sauce mixture. Spoon the sauce over the partially broiled lobster halves and broil slowly until the lobster meat from the shells is done. Take out of the broiler and dust with the cheese … return to the broiler and lightly brown the cheese, Serve immediately (Serves 8)

Cranky's Lobster Newburg

8 lobster tails (8-10 ounces each)
1 large onion (finely chopped)
1 stick butter
1 ½ cups Cranky's Fish Stock
1 cup Madeira
2 cups heavy cream
½ tsp. sea salt
½ tsp. cayenne pepper (ground)
1 tsp. Cranky's Glace de Viande
1 tsp. paprika
4-5 tbsp. lemon juice (freshly squeezed)
1 pound oyster mushrooms (sliced)
3-4 tsp. shallots (chopped)
2 ozs. Cognac
3 tbsp. parsley (freshly chopped)
16 pieces of toast (trimmed and cut as desired)

In a large sauté pan, cook the onions an butter. Split the lobster tails and remove the meat and then cut it into bite size pieces and set aside in a glass bowl. Add the mushrooms to the pan and simmer for about 10-15 minutes. Place all of the other ingredients in the glass bowl with the lobster meat, with the exception of the heavy cream. Toss until all is mixed well and transfer it all to the pan. Cook the mixture until the lobster is almost done. Add the heavy cream and whisk. Bring the mixture to serving temperature, stirring constantly. This will blend in the heavy cream and also serve to thicken the sauce. When the desired thickness is achieved, serve over toast. (Serves 8)

> "Shrimps are good and shrimps are fine, Oh my goodness, they're divine. But cook them fast and cool them quick, Lest these critters turn to brick."

Don't you dare laugh at the use of the word "shrimps." According to "The American Heritage Dictionary," shrimps, is the plural of shrimp and I quote:

"SHRIMP (shrimp) n., pl. shrimp or shrimps. 1. a. any of various small, slender-bodied, chiefly marine decapod crustaceans of the suborder Naranta, most species of which are edible."

Cranky's Shrimp Créole

Shrimp Creole was created before the days of refrigeration, and, like most great dishes, it was made with only fresh ingredients during the season that those ingredients were available. In this case, the whole fresh shrimps and garden ripe tomatoes are the key to the dish. The fat in the shrimp heads is an important and color contributor. Fresh tomatoes and fresh shrimp fat give the sauce a natural sweetness and a wonderful flavor. Browning the onions until caramelized is also an integral part of the dish, as it brings the sugar in the onions to the surface. The use of butter enriches the sauce further and the red and white ground peppers are important stimulators to the taste buds. The completed sauce may have white specks of shrimp fat in it and it should be an antique red in color. The sauce is best if made a day before serving. Make the shrimp stock first, then the sauce. When ready to serve, skim off the oil from the surface and reheat the sauce to a boil. Lower the heat to very low, add the peeled shrimp tails and cook, covered, just until the shrimp shells turn pink or antique red, about 5 minutes.

4 pounds large 16-20 count green shrimp (this means raw with heads and tails and shells and lots of head fat)
3 cups, in all Cranky's Fish Stock
½ cup chicken fat, pork lard or beef lard
3 cups, in all, onions (finely chopped)
2 cups celery (finely chopped)
2 cups sweet green peppers (finely chopped)
4 tbsp. butter (unsalted)
6-8 cloves garlic (minced)
2-4 bay leaves (crushed)
2 tsp. sea salt
1 ½ tsp. white pepper (freshly ground)
1 tsp. black pepper (freshly ground)
1 ½ tsp. Tabasco sauce
2 tbsp. thyme leaves (freshly chopped)
1 tbsp. Basil (freshly chopped)
2 tbsp. sugar
3 cups tomatoes (peeled, seeded and chopped)
2 cups Cranky's Tomato Sauce
8-12 cups cooked white rice
4 cups Cranky's Créole Sauce

Rinse and peel and devein the shrimp and refrigerate until needed. Use the shells and the heads to make the basic shrimp stock. Boil the heads and shells with about 2 quarts of water for about two hours. When done. Add the fish stock and reduce to a total of three to four cups. This will be rich and wonderful. Heat the fat over a high heat and add one cup of the onions and cook to a golden brown and almost caramelized. Add the rest of the onions, celery, peppers and butter. Cook for an additional 5-6 minutes. Add the garlic, the bay leaves, salt, white and black pepper and stir well. Add the Tabasco sauce, thyme, basil, and one cup of the reduced fish/shrimp stock. Cook over medium for about five minutes to allow the vegetables and the flavors to marry. Do not let the mixture stick to the bottom of the pot. Add the tomatoes and cook for ten more minutes, keeping the bottom of the pan clean. Stir in the rest of the shrimp/fish stock and simmer for 5-10 minutes. Add the rest of the fish/shrimp stock and the sugar. Simmer the sauce for 15 more minutes. If serving immediately, turn the heat off and add the shrimp, cover the pot and let it sit until the shrimp are plump and pink ... about ten minutes. Meanwhile, heat the serving plates, place a cup of cooked rice on the plate and flatten out. Pour 1 cup of the créole sauce over the cooked rice and arrange equal portions of the shrimp on top of the sauce. (Serves 8) *1

*1-Save the mixture that you cooked the shrimp in for future use to make a soup, a fish stew ... use your imagination!

Cranky's Shrimp Victoria

2 pounds 16-20 raw shrimp (peeled and deveined)
1 large onion (finely chopped)
1 cup butter
1 pound of mushrooms (sliced)
3 tbsp. flour
1 tsp. sea salt
¼ tsp. cayenne pepper
1 cup heavy cream
1 cups sour cream
6-8 cups cooked rice

Place the butter in a skillet and sauté the mushrooms and the onions for 5-6 minutes. Add the shrimp and cook until the shrimp are pink and plump. Do not overcook. Sprinkle in the flour, salt and cayenne pepper. Stir in the sour cream and the heavy cream alternately and cook slowly, stirring constantly for about 12-15 minutes or until the sauce is creamy smooth. Serve on heated platters over cooked rice.

Cranky's Shrimp Bayou

1½ quarts water
2 pounds 21-25 count raw shrimp in the shell
½ cup olive or vegetable oil
1 cup celery (finely chopped)
½ cup chili sauce

3 tbsp. lemon juice (freshly squeezed)
1 green onion (finely chopped)
2 tbsp. Cranky's Hot Like Hell Horseradish
1 tbsp. Cranky's Hot Like Hell Mustard
½ tsp. paprika
½ tsp. sea salt
Dash of hot sauce of your choice, if necessary

Bring the water to a boil, add the shrimp and cook for 3-5 minutes Drain well and rinse with cold water. Peel and devein the shrimp and set aside. Combine all of the remaining ingredients and stir well. Add the shrimp, toss vigorously and cover in a glass bowl. Chill for about eight hours or overnight. (Serves 8) *1

*1-Can be used as an entrée, a salad or an appetizer.

Cranky's 16 Boy Shrimp Curry

The reason for the name: a different servant brought a different part of the dish to the table and they are all listed below.

1 cup butter
4 pounds 21-25 medium shrimp (peeled and deveined)
4 tbsp. onions (chopped)
4 tbsp. celery (chopped)
4 tbsp. carrots (chopped)
2 cloves garlic (minced)
2 bay leaves (crushed)
5 cups Cranky's Béchamel Sauce
1 cup heavy cream
5 tbsp. curry powder
1 tsp. sea salt
½ tsp. black pepper (freshly ground)
2 tbsp. paprika
2 tsp. coriander (crushed)
2 tsp. cumin
2 quarts cooked rice.

Item to be served separately:

1 portion Rice
1 portion Shrimp
1 portion Sauce
1 cup peanuts (chopped)
1 cup coconut (grated)
1 cup chutney
1 cup watermelon rind (pickled)
1 cup orange rind (grated)
1 cup raisins (white)
1 cup eggs (chopped)
1 cup parsley (freshly chopped)
1 cup ginger (candied)
1 cup almonds (chopped or sliced)
1 cup chives (freshly snipped)
¼ cup nutmeg (freshly ground)
¼ cup cinnamon (ground)

In a large kettle, melt the butter and sauté the shrimp, onion, celery, garlic, and the bay leaves. When the shrimp start to curl, remove them from the vegetables. Add the Béchamel sauce, stirring in the curry powder, salt, pepper, coriander, cumin and paprika ... whisking constantly. Thicken the sauce with the cream. Put the rice, shrimp and the sauce in three large heated bowls. If you do not have 16 servants ... just put the other condiments in separate bowls and let your guests go to town and build their own platefuls of delight. (Serves 8)

Cranky's Abalone with Olive Oil and Butter

While sitting in my favorite cocktail Lounge, I overlooked a conversation dealing with the delicately delicious flesh of the abalone ... especially fresh abalone. It seemed that the talkers were blaming the industrious little sea otter for the abalone's demise. This didn't surprise me at all ... through the ages we have ... mankind ... blamed some other creature for the harm done or the demise of another species. Well, mankind caused the demise of the abalone and not because of their appetite or their need for the meat ... it was the shells for jewelry, brooches, hair devices, inlay for wood carvings, inlays for furniture, belt buckles and, of course, *buttons. The shells were sought after by the rich and famous because of their rich, beautiful, iridescent blues, pinks and greens that grace the ear lobes of many a beautiful woman, dating back to primitive man. Maori Indians used them to inlay their wood carvings and many of the islanders of the Pacific Ocean made some of the best fishing lures ever known to man, in the shape of spoons ... some experts believe that they are the earliest known fishing lures. Most of the desired species of abalone are found along the western coast of the United State, especially of the coast of California. In the latter part of the 19th century, we shipped tons of abalone in the shell and the abalone shells to China and Japan and the shells were selling for many times the value of the abalone meat. Most of the meat was discarded ... hence the cost going up. Thanks to some regulatory laws in California and the United States, fresh abalone in the shell can not be shipped out of the United States. Only canned or dried abalone meat is allowed to be shipped out of the states, as well as, fresh or frozen abalone. That can be only done on a limited basis and with an export or an import license. How about that! If you are lucky to have a friend in California, who is traveling to your area of the country, treat the fresh abalone he brings you with reverence ... do not overcool ... it will get only get very chewy and tough. Do not overcook, do not beat it too long ... it will only become dry, tasteless and tough as leather. I never cook abalone for more that 20-25 seconds per side ... just like other mollusks ... overcooking will only toughen the flesh.*

4 large abalone steaks
1 cup flour
2-3 eggs (beaten)
1 tsp. sea salt
1 tsp. black pepper (freshly ground)
1 cup olive oil
1 cup butter (unsalted)
1 lemon (freshly squeezed)
1 tbsp. parsley (freshly chopped)
1-2 lemons (wedged)

Tenderize the abalone steaks until they are one fourth inch thick, cutting them into halves. Dry mix the flour, salt and pepper on a flat pan. Dip the steaks in the beaten egg and dust with the flour mixture. Repeat the procedure and sauté the steaks in a mixture of half butter and half olive oil. Brown the steaks on both sides ... about 45-50 seconds per side. Place the steaks on heated platters. Pour the oil out of the pan and melt the remaining butter.

Cook the butter until it is light brown, adding the lemon juice and the parsley. Pour this over the abalone and serve with the lemon wedges and a good white wine. (Serves 8)

Cranky's Scampi Supreme

1 cup butter
4 green onions (chopped)
4 stalks celery (chopped)
2 carrots (scrapped and chopped)
¼ tsp. oregano (freshly chopped)
½ tsp. thyme (freshly chopped)
4 pounds fresh scampi (6-10 count)
½ cup white wine
½ cup Cognac
3 cups heavy cream
1 cup milk
½ cup dry sherry
1 tsp. sea salt
1 tsp. black pepper (freshly ground)
2 tsp. lemon juice (freshly squeezed)
1 cup butter
½ cup parsley (freshly chopped)
1 cup Parmesan cheese (freshly grated)

To a large skillet add the butter, onions, celery, carrots, oregano and the thyme. Sauté for ten minutes, add the scampi that have been split down the back and deveined and sauté for 5-6 minutes longer, adding the wine gradually and tossing frequently. Add the Cognac and ignite. When the fire is out … remove the scampi. Add the cream, sherry, milk salt pepper and lemon juice. Heat and thicken with the butter and flour roux to the consistency of cream. Strain the sauce. Place the scampi into small casseroles. Swirl in the butter and the parsley and pour the mixture over the scampi. Sprinkle the Parmesan cheese on top and heat for 2-3 minutes in a very hot over. Serve immediately. (Serves 8)

Cranky's Paella Valençiana

½ cup olive oil
1-3 pound chicken (cut into 8 pieces)
1 pound of pork
1 pound of veal
1 pound of Italian sausage
2-4 cloves garlic (minced)
2 medium onions (sliced) 1 tsp. sea salt
2 tsp. black pepper (freshly ground)
1 pound of tomatoes (peeled, seeded and chopped)
4 cups Cranky's Chicken Stock
8-9 cups Cranky's Wild Rice Basic Preparation
1 sweet green pepper (chopped)
1 cup peas
2 cups artichoke hearts
1 tsp. saffron
1 pound lump crabmeat
1 pound lobster meat
16 medium shrimp (shell on)
16 live cherrystones (scrubbed)
16 live mussels (scrubbed and bearded)
1 cup of water
1 cup white wine
4 lemons (wedged)
2-4 tbsp. parsley (freshly chopped)

Soak the saffron in some white wine. In a large and deep kettle, place the olive oil with the chicken, pork, veal, sausage, and cook until all parts are golden brown. Add the garlic, onion, salt, pepper and tomatoes and simmer for fifteen minutes. Add the saffron, green pepper, peas and artichoke hearts. If you are using fresh peas … put them into the pot about ten minutes earlier. Frozen peas work as well. Add the crabmeat, lobster meat and the shrimp and simmer for one minute. When all is almost dome, place the clams and mussels on top. Add the wine and the water. Cover. Simmer until all of the mollusks are open. Place the chicken on a large serving platter. Cover with the paella and circle the dish with the open mussels and clams. Garnish with the lemon and parsley. (Serves 8)

Cranky's Crayfish Étouffée

5-6 pounds crayfish meat (raw)
½ pound butter
4 cloves garlic (minced)
1 large onion (chopped)
½ cup celery (chopped)
½ cup sweet green pepper (chopped)
4-5 shallots (chopped)
½ tsp sea salt
1 tsp. black pepper (freshly ground)
2 tbsp. parsley (freshly chopped)
1 tsp. thyme (freshly chopped)
1 tsp. basil (freshly chopped)
4 cups Cranky's Fish Stock
4-6 cups cooked rice
½ cup Cranky's Golden Roux

In a large skillet, melt the butter and sauté the garlic, the onions, celery, green peppers and the shallots. Add the salt, pepper, parsley, thyme and the basil and stir well. Add the raw crayfish meat and simmer for 6-7 minutes. Heat the fish stock and stir into the skillet. Thicken the mixture with the roux, making sure that it is thinner than the average sauce. Smother over the cooked rice. (Serves 8)

Cranky's Crayfish and Beer Rice

8 pounds live crayfish
3-4 quarts Cranky's Fish Stock
8-10 cups Cranky's Beer Rice
1 recipe Cranky's Crab Boil Mixture
½ cup parsley (freshly chopped)
½ cup arrowroot
Sea salt to taste
Black pepper (freshly ground)
½ cup parsley (freshly chopped)
2-3 loaves of Cranky's Garlic Bread
Olive oil

½ cup parsley (freshly chopped)
2-3 lemons (wedged)

Put the fish stock and the crab boil mixture in a large kettle and cook the crayfish until they are pink to red in color. Remove the crayfish from the liquid and tear off the tails and set aside. Place the heads and the small legs and the smaller claw in cloth bag and crush with the flat side of a cleaver. The large claws should be frozen, and when you get some time, pick the meat out and it will make a delicious crayfish cocktail, or, if you save enough, a crayfish étouffée. Return to the liquid, simmer and let reduce to half volume. Strain through some cheesecloth and make sure all of the shell pieces have been removed. Thicken the sauce with the arrowroot and season with the salt and pepper. Remove the tails from the shells, devein and fold into the sauce. Place a ring of beer rice on heated plates and ladle the crayfish and the sauce over the rice. Garnish with the parsley and serve with the hot garlic bread on the side and lemon wedges. (Serves 8)

Cranky's French Coins or Pouched Scallop Medallions in Lobster Sauce

This recipe was called French Coins at one time because of the appearance of the scallop medallions after they are poached in a court bouillon containing saffron. For best results, the saffron should be soaked overnight which releases more of the yellow color.

3-4 pounds sea scallops
1-2 quarts Cranky's Court Bouillon
1 cup butter
1 cup shallots (freshly chopped)
4-6 cups Cranky's Cardinal Sauce
½-1 oz. saffron
1 cup red wine
½ tsp. sea salt
½ tsp. black pepper (freshly ground)
2 tbsp. parsley (freshly chopped)
8 small red tea roses

Trim the large muscles from the sides of the scallops and slice in ¼ inch slices against the grain. Leave them in their liquor and set aside. Leave the scallops in their own liquid and set aside. In a 3-4 quart saucepan, place the shallots and the butter and sauté until translucent. During this time, dissolve the saffron in the white wine and after about three to four hours, add the court bouillon and the saffron liquid to the pan, the scallop liquor and the scallop scraps ... not the muscles. Bring the mixture to a slow simmer ... salt and pepper to taste. Heat the Cardinal sauce and pour a ladle full into heated soup dishes. Wrap the scallop medallions gently in the court bouillon liquid for about one minute. Remove the medallions and place equal numbers of the medallions in a circular pattern on top of the sauce in the soup dishes. Garnish with a red tea rose and sprinkle chopped parsley sparingly on the top of the dish. (Serves 8)

Cranky's Scallops with Glazed Garlic and Champagne Sauce

12 large garlic cloves (each cut in half)
4 tbsp. butter
40 large sea scallops
Sea salt to taste
Black pepper to taste (freshly ground)
¼ cup pure maple syrup
¼ cup apple cider
¼ cup Champagne
3 tbsp. shallots (chopped)
3 tbsp chives (freshly snipped)

Place the garlic in a small saucepan of water. Bring to a boil, Drain. Return the garlic to the pan. Add fresh water, bring to a boil again. Drain and set aside. Melt the butter in a large skillet over high heat. Season the scallops with the salt and pepper. Sauté the scallops until cooked through ... toss the scallops often. Using some tongs, transfer the scallops to a heated platter and keep warm. Without cleaning the skillet, add the garlic, maple syrup, apple cider to it and reduce to a glaze. It takes about three minutes. Add Champagne, shallots and the chives, Add the remaining butter and whisk until it is slightly thicker. Season with the salt and pepper and pour over the scallops. Sprinkle with the remaining chives and serve immediately. (Serves 8)

Cranky's Stir-Fried Scallops with Rice

1-8 oz. package of long-grained rice pilaf mix
3 cups broccoli (chopped and cooked)
1 pound sea scallops
1 medium sweet red pepper
1 tbs. olive oil
½ tsp. sea salt
¼ tsp. white pepper (freshly ground)
2 tsp. lemon juice (freshly squeezed)

Prepare the rice pilaf as the instructions state. When the pilaf is done, stir in the broccoli and heat the mixture through completely. Rinse the scallops and thinly slice the red pepper. Sauté the red pepper and the scallops in the oil until the scallops are opaque. Toss the mixture often. Stir in the lemon juice and salt and pepper to taste, Place a ring of pilaf on heated plates and spoon the scallop mixture on top of the pilaf. (Serves 8)

Cranky's Scallops Flamed with Cognac

3 pounds sea scallops (muscled removed, rinsed and halved)
1 tsp. sea salt
½ tsp. black pepper (freshly ground)
1 cup butter
4 tbsp. Cognac (heated)
2 lemons (wedged)

Put the scallops in a saucepan with the salt and pepper and some waters and poach them lightly or until they are opaque. Drain. In a skillet, melt the butter over moderately high heat. Add the scallops and sauté until they are golden brown. Pour in the Cognac and ignite and toss until the flame is extinguished. Transfer the scallops to the dishes, pour the liquid over themand garnish with the lemon wedges (Serves 8)

Cranky's Scallops in Cardinal Sauce

40-48 sea scallops (muscles removed)
1 pound of sliced bacon
3-4 cups Cranky's Fish Stock

½ medium onion (finely chopped)
16 small potatoes (peeled)
16 mushrooms of your choice
16 pearl onions
2 tbsp. parsley (freshly chopped)
½ cup butter
8 skewers
4 cups Cranky's Saffron Rice
2-3 cups Cranky's Cardinal Sauce (heated)
2 lemons (wedged)

Cut the bacon in lengths and stretch them out. Cook until one half done. Bring the fish stock to a simmer and cook the onions for ten minutes, add the peeled potatoes and the mushrooms and cook until almost done. Strain and allow the vegetable to cool. Wrap each scallop with or in a strip of bacon and place on the skewers, alternating with a pearl onion, a potato and a mushroom so that each skewer has 7 scallops, 2 potatoes, 2 mushrooms and 2 pearl onions. Make a mixture of the parsley and the butter and brush the skewers. Broil until the scallops are cooked to a light golden brown and still moist. Serve the skewers on beds of saffron rice and smother with the hot Cardinal sauce. (Serves 8)

Cranky's Chili-Garlic Scallops

4 tbsp. butter
3 pounds sea scallops (muscles removed and cut in half cross grain)
2 cloves garlic (minced)
1-2 jalapeño pepper (seeded and minced)
½ tsp. turmeric
6 tbsp water
½ cup cilantro (freshly chopped finely)
Sea salt to taste

Heat the butter in a large skillet and brown lightly, Remove the scallops and set them aside. Add the garlic to the skillet and cook for 1-2 minutes. Stir in the pepper and the turmeric. Add the water and bring to a boil. Add the scallops, reduce the heat and simmer with a cover until the scallops are opaque. Using a slotted spoon, remove the scallops to a heated platter and reduce the liquid to about one half. Stir in the cilantro with salt to taste. Pour this over the scallops and serve immediately. (Serves 8)

Cranky's Scallops and Grapes

4 tbsp. olive oil
3-4 pounds sea scallops (muscles removed)
1 cup slivered almonds
2 cups dry white wine
1 pound red grapes (seedless)
1 pound white grapes (seedless)
4 tbsp. butter
4 tbsp. parsley (freshly chopped)

Brown the almonds in the oven. Heat the olive oil in a large skillet, adding the scallops and braising them to a golden brown. Toss them frequently. Remove them to a glass bowl. Add the white wine to the skillet, reduce to one half. Add the almonds, grapes, butter and parsley. Bring back to a simmer. Add the scallops, toss to coat everything and serve on heated plates immediately. (Serve 8)

Cranky's Mixed Seafood Bag

8 ounces red snapper (fresh)
8 ounces tuna (fresh)
16 sea scallops (trimmed)
16 shrimp (peeled and deveined)
16 mushrooms of your choice (sliced)
16 asparagus spears (cut into 1 inch pieces)
2 carrots (scrapped and julienne)
2 shallots (finely chopped)
1-2 cups dry white wine
4 tsp. Dijon mustard
2 tsp. marjoram (freshly chopped)
1 tsp. thyme (freshly chopped)
2 tsp. parsley (freshly chopped)
½ tsp. sea salt
½ tsp. black pepper (freshly ground)

¼ tsp. white pepper (freshly ground)
2 cups Cranky's Clam Juice
¼ pound butter
8 cups Cranky's Saffron Rice

Cut the red snapper and the tuna into bite sized pieces and place them in a large glass bowl. Add all of the rest of the ingredients to the bowl, except the rice, and toss like a salad. Chill for 2-3 hours and let everything marinate. Lay a large piece of cheesecloth over the top part of a steamer and place everything in the cheesecloth with the clam juice and the butter in the bottom of the steamer. Tie the cheesecloth together and place the lid on the steamer. Steam everything for about 15-17 minutes or until the tuna is done. When finished, transfer the bag to a large bowl, untie the cheesecloth, pour the contents of the pot over the vegetables and the seafood and serve with the saffron rice. (Serves 8)

Cranky's Curried Mussels

5-6 quarts live mussels (scrubbed and bearded)
¼ cup olive oil
1 cup onion (minced)
2 cloves garlic (minced)
Cranky's Bouquet Garni III
1 cup butter
2 cups dry white wine
4 tsp. flour
4 tsp. curry powder
1 cup heavy cream
Lemon juice to taste
Sea salt to taste
Black pepper to taste (freshly ground)

In a large kettle, with a little oil, cook 3 teaspoons of the onions, the garlic and the Bouguet Garni, along with the butter. Add the mussels and the wine and bring the liquid to a boil. Increase the heat to high and steam the mussels. Discard the unopened mussels. Shell the mussels and keep them warm. Strain the liquid in the kettle and reduce the liquid to 1 ½ cups. In a saucepan, cook the remaining onion and butter over moderate heat until they are translucent.

Stir in the flour and cook the roux for about 2 minutes. Ad the curry powder and cook for one minute. Remove the pan from heat, pour in the hot mussel liquid, whisking vigorously until mixture is thick and smooth. Simmer the sauce for about 5 minutes. Stir in the heavy cream, the lemon juice, the salt and the pepper to taste. Add the reserved mussels and heat them. Serve on a rice or noodle of your choice. (Serves 8)

Cranky's Mussels in Tomato Sauce

1 tbsp olive oil
1 tbsp. garlic (minced)
1 tbsp fresh ginger (grated)
1 tsp. jalapeño pepper (seeded and chopped)
½ tsp. cumin (ground)
½ tsp. turmeric
½ pound plum tomatoes (peeled and chopped)
½ cup water
4 pounds live mussels (scrubbed and bearded)
Sea salt to taste
1-2 tsp. cilantro (freshly chopped)

Heat the oil in a kettle over low heat. Add the garlic and the ginger and cook until golden, stirring often to prevent sticking. Add the jalapeño, cumin and turmeric and stir to distribute evenly. Stir in the tomatoes and the water. Bring to a boil, reduce the heat and simmer, covered, until a thick sauce forms…. 15 minutes perhaps. During this process, uncover and smash the tomatoes to help form the sauce. Discard any opened or broken mussels. Raise the heat and add the mussels, cover the pan and cook the mussels for about five or ten minutes or until all of the mussels are open. Discard the unopened mussels and season with the salt and the cilantro, serving the mussels and the sauce in large heated bowls. (Serves 8)

Cranky's Mussels with Leeks, Saffron and Cream

2 tbsp. butter
2 large leeks (sliced white and pale green parts)
8 dozen live mussels (scrubbed and bearded)
1 cup dry white wine

8 fresh parsley sprigs
10 saffron threads
½ cup heavy cream
2 tbsp. parsley (freshly minced)
Sea salt to taste
Black pepper to taste (freshly ground)

Melt the butter in a large heavy and deep skillet. Add the leeks and sauté them until tender. Combine the mussels, wine and the parsley sprigs and steam open. Transfer the mussels to a glass bowl, discarding any that are not open. Strain the mussel juices into the skillet containing the leeks. Add the saffron and cream to the skillet and whisk briskly. Simmer until the liquid reduced to a smooth sauce. Stir in the minced parsley and season with the salt and pepper. Add the mussels and any accumulated juices to the skillet. Stir over low heat until heated through. Divide into large heated bowls. Pour the sauce over the mussels. (Serves 8)

Cranky's Mussels with Mop Sauce

8 pounds live mussels, scrubbed and bearded)
1-2 quarts Cranky's Mop Sauce
3-4 loaves French bread
1 cup olive oil
I cup Parmesan cheese

Place the mussels in a large kettle and pour the mop sauce over them. Cover and steam the mussels open. Discard the unopened ones. Serve in large heated bowls and dust them with the Parmesan cheese, accompanied with the French bread sliced and dipped in olive oil or garlic bread if preferred. (Serves 8)

Cranky's Mussels with Fines Herbes

8 pounds live mussels (scrubbed and bearded)
4 cups dry white wine
1 large onion (finely chopped)
4 cloves garlic (minced)
3 tbsp basil (freshly chopped)
3 tbsp. parsley (freshly chopped)

2 tbsp lemon juice (freshly squeezed)
1 tsp. sea salt
1 tsp. white pepper (freshly ground)
5-6 tbsp. butter

Place them in a deep stew pot along with all of the other ingredients. Cover and cook until all of the mussels are open. Discard any of the unopened mussels. Separate the mussels into heated soup bowls. Strain the broth into another saucepan and reduce over high heat by one third. Ladle the thickened broth over the mussels and serve at once. (Serves)

Cranky's Barbequed Mussels

8 pounds of mussels (scrubbed and bearded)
3-4 cups Cranky's Sensational BBQ Sauce
2 pounds bacon (thick slices)
2 cups sweet pepper (cut into one inch squares)
2 cups button mushroom caps
2 cups pearl onions (cooked)
2-3 loaves of French bread
½ cup olive oil
½ cup Parmesan cheese

Open the mussels on the BBQ and remove from the shells. Thread the mussels on skewers alternately with the green pepper squares, the pearl onions and the button mushrooms. Brush the skewers liberally with the BBQ sauce and place at the edge of the coals. Turn them often and at the same time brushing them again and again with the rest of the sauce. Remove from the fire and serve at once on a bed of a rice recipe of your choice and a great deal of beer or wine and French bread that you have dipped in olive oil and dusted with parmesan cheese. (Serves 8)

Cranky's Little Neck Clams with Mop Sauce

8-10 pounds live little clams (scrubbed)
1-2 quarts Cranky's Mop Sauce
2 cups butter
1 cup olive oil

3-4 loaves French bread
2-3 lemons (wedged)

Place the clams in a large kettle and pour the Mop Sauce over them. Cover the kettle and bring to a boil until all of the clams are opened. Slice the bread and serve the clams in heated bowls with the olive oil on the side, a side dish of Mop Sauce and a side dish of melted butter. (Serves 8)

Cranky's Clams in Sherry and Black Beans Sauce

10-12 cherrystones per person
2 tbsp. olive oil
2 large shallots (minced)
2 garlic cloves (minced)
½ cup dry sherry
2 tsp. sugar
1 tsp. black pepper (freshly ground)
2 tsp. black beans (cooked and blended smooth)
2 tsp. Cranky's Salsa Rosa
4 large scallions (thinly sliced)
2 loaves French bread

Cook the shallots in the oil for about a minute, add the garlic and stir. Add the sherry, sugar and pepper and simmer for one more minute. Stir in the bean mixture and the salsa. Add the clams to the pot and cover … shaking often … until the clams open. Divide the clams and the sauce into heated bowls and serve with French bread. (Serves 8)

Cranky's Fried Smelts

5-6 pounds fresh smelts
1 ½ quarts vegetable oil
3-4 cups flour
1 tsp. sea salt
1 tsp. black pepper (freshly ground)
1-2 eggs (beaten and diluted with ½ cup water)
3-4 cups milk
½ cups parsley (freshly chopped)

2-3 lemons (wedged)
2 cups Cranky's Tartar Sauce

Heat the oil in a large deep pot so that the oil doesn't boil over and catch fire. Soak the smelt in the milk that has been salted and peppered. Roll each smelt in the flour and drop into the hot oil. Cook until crisp but not past light or golden brown. Serve them on some paper towels with the parsley sprinkled and the lemon wedges and tartar sauce on the side. (Serves 8)

Cranky's Squid and Greens

2 pounds each of collards and kale or any combination of greens that you prefer
10 tbsp. olive oil
2 tsp. garlic (minced)
2-4 cloves garlic (crushed)
8 squid steaks (3-4 pounds)
2-3 cups flour
1-2 eggs (beaten and cut with ½ cup water)
2-3 cups flour
2-3 bread crumbs
Sea salt to taste
Black pepper (freshly ground)
¼ cup parsley (freshly chopped)
4 lemons (wedged)

Cook the greens in some salted water and when the stems are tender, drain the greens and chop them, stems and all. Heat some olive oil in a large skillet and add the minced garlic. Through in the chopped greens and toss them briskly and remove them to a heated serving platter. Heat the rest of the oil in the skillet. Toss in the garlic clove and at the same time dredge the steaks in the flour, then the egg mixture and then the bread crumbs. Cook the steaks quickly over medium heat, about two minutes per steak or a light golden brown. Place the steaks on top of the greens, sprinkle with the chopped parsley. Sprinkle with the cheese and put the platter in the oven for about 1 minute. Serve with parsley sprinkled on top of the steaks and the lemon wedges. (Serves 8)

Cranky's Dungeness Crab

This is a favorite at my house and a delicious surprise to your seafood loving guests. No formality here ... roll up the sleeves, tap that keg, bring out the frosted glasses and have lots of lemon wedges and paper towels.

8-2 pound live Dungeness crabs
2 whole bunches of dill
3 tsp. sea salt
3-4 carrots (scrapped and chopped)
2 large onions (chopped)
½ cup parsley (freshly chopped)
3-4 bay leaves
10-15 black peppercorns
4 egg yolks
1 cup olive oil
3-4 tsp. lemon juice (freshly squeezed)
2 tsp. Dijon mustard
1 tsp. sea salt
1 tsp. black pepper (freshly ground)
3-4 lemons (wedged)

In a very large kettle, place the crabs and all of the ingredients through the peppercorns. Save some of the dill tips for the sauce. Cover with water bring to a boil and cook for 20 minutes. Take off the stove and allow to cool. Place all of the rest of the ingredients, plus the dill tips and except the lemon wedges, in a food processor and process until it is smooth and creamy. Take the crabs from the pot and allow them drain. Tear off the back skirt and discard. Lift the top shell or carapace off of the body and set aside. In a glass bowl, reserve the milky yellow substance in the center of the body and add to the blender, along with the liver from the main shell and blend again until smooth. Chill for at least 2-3 hours. Wash the crab shells inside and out and place them in the freezer. Rinse the bodies with the legs and claws attached under cold water and chill well in the refrigerator. After the cocktails and the proper hors d'oeuvres have been consumed serve each guest a crab on a large dinner plate with the carapaces returned to the original position. Put the sauce in a clean glass bowl with a small ladle. Have plenty of lemon wedges and good pairs of crackers and paper towels on hand. Ladle some sauce into shell that you have removed and set upside down in front of your plate. Have some large bowls for shells. (Serves 8)

Cranky's Crab Legs Saute

8-10 pounds king crab legs
4 tbsp. vegetable oil
2 cups half and half
2 cups flour
2 lemons (peeled and chopped)
4 tbsp. parsley (freshly chopped)
2 tbsp. capers (chopped)
4 large mushrooms of choice
1 small onion (chopped)
½ pound butter
2-3 lemons (wedged)

Carefully take the meat out of the crab shells and cut them into bite size pieces. Put them into a glass bowl and cover them with the half and half. Let this sit for about 30 minutes. Pat the pieces dry and roll the pieces in the flour. Saute for 2-3 minutes in very hot oil until they are a light golden brown. Place on a serving platter and keep hot in a 200 degree oven. Melt the butter and saute the chopped lemons, parsley, capers, onions and the mushrooms for 2-4 minutes on low heat so that the butter never burns. Pour this liquid over the crab pieces and serve immediately. (Serves 8)

Cranky's Crab Boil

48 Maryland Blue Claw Crabs
4 cups Cranky's Crab Boil Mixture
24 small new potatoes
2-3 large onions (peeled)
30-40 whole cloves
8 ears of sweet corn

In a very large kettle, put 3-4 gallons of water and add the crab boil mixture. Bring to a boil and add the three onions that have been pierced with the whole cloves, new potatoes and the corn. Bring back to a boil and cook for 6-8 minutes. Dump in the crabs, live and wiggly and bring back to a boil and cook for 6-8 minutes more. Everything will come out well-seasoned and delicious. These crabs can be served hot or cold … I prefer them to be ice cold. (Serves 8-10

Cranky's Crab Rice

1 cup sweet green pepper (chopped)
2 green onions (chopped with the greens
1 habanero (seeded and chopped)
2 cloves garlic (minced)
3 cups uncooked rice
5-6 tbsp. olive oil
6-7 tomatoes (peeled, seeded and chopped)
4 tbsp. Cranky's Tomato paste
2 tsp. oregano (freshly chopped)
4 bay leaves
3 cups lump crabmeat (cooked)
4 cups Cranky's Chicken Stock
2 cups dry white wine
4 tbsp. parsley (freshly chopped)

Sauté all of the vegetables in the olive oil in a large deep skillet. Add the uncooked rice and brown slightly. Place this mixture in a large Dutch oven and add the tomato paste, oregano, chicken stock, oregano and the bay leaves. Cover and simmer for 30 minutes. When the rice is done, add the crabmeat and the white wine. Bring to serving temperature. Fluff the rice, remove the bay leaves and serve in hot bowls, and garnish with the chopped parsley. (Serves 8)

Cranky's Softshell Crabs

If I were to have a choice for a last meal on my deathbed, it would be this dish. The most important procedure in the preparation of the softshell crabs is the initial cleaning and proper treatment of this delicate little animal.

16 live and wiggle soft-shell crab
8 English muffins

1-2 pound butter
1 tsp. black pepper (freshly ground)
1 cup dry white wine
2 tbsp. lemon juice (freshly squeezed)
1 tsp. chervil (freshly chopped)
2 tsp. paprika
2 cups Cranky's Tartar Sauce

To prepare live softshell crabs:

Turn the crabs over and, with a sharp pair of kitchen scissors, remove the back flaps. Flip the ends of the shells up and cut away the spongy gills or lungs. Turn the flaps down again. Cut about ¼ inch of the front part of the crab away just behind the eyes. Squeeze the crab between your thumb and forefinger until the air bubble pops out. Tear this sac out and throw away. You are now ready to cook the softshells.

Sauté the soft shells crabs in a large skillet on very low heat in the butter and the paprika. When they are reddish on both sides, add the wine, chervil and the lemon juice and flame the mixture. Toast the English Muffins and butter them and then spread the tartar sauce on the buns. Place a soft shell crab on each English muffin half. Add the cream to the pan and whisk briskly until nice and smooth and pour this over the crabs. (Serves 8)

Cranky's Softshell Crabs with Fig Fritters

24 figs (dried)
12 almonds (shelled and blanched)
1 cup pine nuts
2 cups red wine (heated)
1 tsp cinnamon (ground)
4-5 cloves
1 Double recipe Cranky's Fritter Batter
2 quarts vegetable oil
16 live soft shell crabs (prepared as in Cranky's Soft Shell Crab recipe)
2-3 lemons (wedged)
½ cup parsley (freshly chopped)

Place the figs in a steamer or in a strainer over a pot of boiling water. Cover and steam for about 30 minutes or until the figs are completely soft. Stuff the figs with an almond and a few pine nuts. Place the figs in a glass bowl and cover with the heated red wine, adding the cinnamon and the cloves. Steep the figs for about twenty minutes. Strain the figs, drink the wine ... I never waste a thing ... and pat dry the figs. Dip the figs into the fritter batter and deep fry until golden, Drain and keep warm until the crabs are cooked. Prepare the crabs as in Cranky's Soft Shell Crab recipe, dip them in the fritter batter, and fry a few at a time, drain them on a piece of brown paper or on paper towels. Serve them on heated plates with the fig fritters and a couple of lemon wedges and some chopped parsley. (Serves 8)

Cranky's Charcoal Broiled Soft Shell Crabs

16 live soft shell crabs (prepared as in Cranky's Soft Shell Crabs recipe)
1cup Cranky's Tomato Sauce
1 cup white wine
2-3 cloves garlic (minced)
3-4 tbsp. parsley (freshly chopped)
1 tsp. tarragon (freshly chopped)
1 tsp lemon juice(freshly squeezed)
1 tsp. sea salt
1 tsp. black pepper (freshly ground)
1 cup butter (melted)

Prepare the crabs as in Cranky's Soft Shell Crabs recipe. Place the crabs in a large oblong casserole and add the tomato sauce, white wine, garlic, parsley, tarragon, lemon juice, salt and black pepper. Chill for 2-3 hours. Take the crabs out of the marinade and broil over moderately hot coals for about 2 minutes a side ... 3-4 minutes if you like the cabs very crisp. Remember to use the marinade frequently. Keep enough of the marinade to reduce and use as a wonderful tangy sauce that you should serve on the side. I like to serve this dish on toast that you have buttered and trimmed or English muffins that you have buttered. (Serves 8)

Cranky's Softshell Crabs in Saffron and Pernod

16-24 live soft shell crabs

1-2 quarts Cranky's Fish Stock
6-10 strands saffron (soaked in 2 ounces of white wine)
1-2 ounces Pernod
½ tsp. sea salt
½ tsp. black pepper (freshly ground)
1 cup half and half
2-3 tbsp arrowroot
½ cup parsley (freshly chopped)
1 tsp. paprika (ground)

Prepare the crabs as in Cranky's Soft Shell Crabs recipe. Poach the crabs for about 6-8 minutes in the fish stock that you have laced with the wine, Pernod and saffron wine. Remove the crabs to a heated platter and bring the liquid to a rolling boil. Reduce the stock and season to your taste with the salt and pepper, Thicken the sauce with the half and half and he arrowroot. Whisk until smooth. Strain over the crabs and garnish with the parsley and the paprika and the lemon wedges. (Serves 8)

POTPOURRI PANACHE

This is a very important part or group of particular pages that I call the potpourri panache that will inform even the most persnickety and particular cook of the perplexing plethoric panorama of pleasing preparations that will pamper any person's pantry.

Cranky's Sauce

4 cups Cranky's Béchamel Sauce
1-2 ounce of black truffles (finely chopped)
4 carrots (scrapped, minced and parboiled)
2 medium onions (minced and parboiled
4 ozs. butter (melted)
Sea salt to taste
Black pepper (freshly ground)

Force the parboiled vegetables through a fine sieve into a sauce pan. Save the vegetable liquid. Add the Bechamel sauce to the puree mixture of wine, truffles, carrots, onions and butter: whisking vigorously. Set aside. Reduce the vegetable liquid to one third cup. Combine both liquids and simmer for 8-10 minutes, stirring constantly. Salt and pepper to taste. (Makes about 1 quart)

Cranky's Cardinal Sauce

4 cups Cranky's Béchamel Sauce
½ cup Cranky's Fish Stock
3-4 ounces lobster meat (minced)
2 tbsp. black truffle (freshly minced)
6-8 tbsp. Cranky's Lobster Butter à la Maison
Sea salt to taste
Black pepper to taste (freshly ground)

This the Béchamel sauce with the fish stock until you achieve the proper thickness. Fold in the lobster meat and the truffles. Salt and pepper the mixture to taste. Just prior to serving, stir in the lobster butter with the heat turned off. (Makes 4-5 cups)

Cranky's Créole Sauce

2 onions (chopped)
4 cloves garlic (minced)
6-8 large tomatoes (peeled, seeded and chopped)
½ cup olive oil
2 tsp. brown sugar
2 tbsp. dark molasses

½ pound okra (stem cut off and chopped)
1 tsp. sea salt
1 tsp. black pepper (freshly ground)
4 tbsp. parsley (freshly chopped)
3-4 dashes Tabasco sauce

Start by slowly pan frying the onions, celery, garlic and the tomatoes in the olive oil. When the onions are translucent, add the sugar and the molasses and cook for 10 minutes. Add the okra, salt, pepper and parsley … simmering until the sauce thickens to the proper consistency. Introduce the Tabasco to taste. (Makes 1½ quarts)

Cranky's Mornay Sauce

4 cups Cranky's Béchamel Sauce
4 egg yolks (beaten)
4 tbsp. Parmesan cheese (melted)
4 tbsp. Gruyere cheese (melted)
6 tbsp. butter (melted)

Beat the eggs and add the butter gradually until smooth. Add this hollandaise base to the Bechamel sauce and stir in the melted cheese in a brisk manner. Serve at once. (Makes approximately 1 quart)

Cranky's Aioli Sauce

5-6 cloves of garlic (minced)
2 egg yolks
8-9 tbsp. olive oil
1 tsp. lemon juice (freshly squeezed)
1 tbsp. cold water
¼ tsp. sea salt
¼ tsp black pepper (freshly ground)

Mince the garlic and blend well with the egg yolks until very creamy. Add the olive oil at few drops at a time until all of the olive oil has been consumed by the egg and garlic mixture. It should thicken. Add the lemon juice and the cold water a little of the time, whisking briskly until they are also absorbed. If the sauce curdles during this process, you can normally save it by adding another egg yolk and whisking like a crazy man into the mixture. Add the salt and pepper. (Makes about ½ cup)

Cranky's Gregoire Sauce

4 cups Cranky's Fish Stock
2 tbsp. shallots (chopped)
5 ozs. mushrooms (chopped)
2 bay leaves (crushed)
¼ oz. thyme (freshly chopped)
2 cups Cranky's White Wine Sauce I
2 cups heavy cream
¼ cup Bearnaise Sauce
2-3 drops of Ricard and Picard
1 tsp. lemon juice (freshly squeezed)

Combine the fish stock, the shallots, the mushrooms, the bay leaves and the thyme. Reduce to one half of the volume. Add the wine sauce and again reduce to half. Replace the reduction with the heavy cream. Simmer for 5 minutes more, then strain through a fine cloth. Just before serving, add the Béarnaise sauce flavored with a few drops of Ricard or Pernod. Correct the flavoring with the lemon juice. (Makes about 4 cups)

Cranky's Béarnaise Sauce

1½ cups tarragon vinegar
4 tbsp shallots (chopped)
4 tbsp. tarragon vinegar
¼ tsp. white pepper (freshly ground)
2 tbsp. cold water
6 egg yolks (beaten and separated from the whites completely)
1 pound butter (clarified)
1 tsp. tarragon (freshly chopped)
1 tsp. parsley (freshly chopped)
1 tsp. chervil (freshly chopped)
Sea salt to taste
Black pepper to taste (freshly ground)

Combine the first four ingredients in a sauce pan and reduce the total to 2 tablespoons. Remove the pan from the heat and add the cold water. Add the egg yolks slowly whisking briskly until the sauce is thick and smooth. Whisk in the clarified butter very slowly. Continue to whisk until as thick as desired. Season the sauce with the salt and the pepper. Whisk in the tarragon and the parsley and remove from the heat. (Makes about 2 pints)

Cranky's Hollandaise Sauce

4 cups butter (melted)
12 egg yolks (beaten in a stainless steel bowl)
1 tsp. sea salt
½ tsp. white pepper (freshly ground)
Lemon juice to taste (freshly squeezed)
Cayenne pepper to taste (ground)

Fill one of your sinks with very hot water. Beat the egg yolks in a cold stainless steel bowl, keeping the bowl spinning in the hot water as you are whisking. Melt the butter and bring it just before a boil. Pour the butter, a little of the time into the beaten eggs into the steel bowl that you have sitting in the hot water in the sink. Continue to add the hot butter to the egg and butter mixture in a continuously adding and beating process. When all of the butter has been added and the sauce is a creamy gold color and very smooth ... have someone add the lemon juice and the salt and the pepper and the cayenne while you are whisking at a steady pace ... all of the time ... keeping the stainless steel bowl in the hot water ... spinning it as often as possible ... this sauce can be done in a double boiler on low heat with great success ... however ... it will never taste like this preparation. (Makes about 2-3 cups of sauce)

Cranky's Béchamel Sauce

2 tbsp onion (minced)
6 tbsp. butter
½ cup flour
5 cups half and half (scalded)
Sea salt to taste
Black pepper to taste (freshly ground)

Sauté the onion in the butter until the onion is translucent. Stir in the flour and cook the roux for about 2 minutes. Remove from the heat and add the milk gradually; stirring vigorously until smooth. Add the salt and pepper to taste and simmer for 5-7 minutes. Strain through a fine sieve and keep warm. (Makes about 1 quart)

Cranky's Velouté Sauce

4 tbsp. onion (minced)
12 tbsp. butter
½ cup flour
4 cups stock (use the appropriate stock)
Sea salt to taste
Black pepper to taste (freshly ground)

Sauté the onions in butter until they are translucent. Stir in the flour and cook the roux slowly over low heat for about 3 minutes. Remove the pan from the heat and add the stock desired. Veal stock for veal … chicken stock for chicken, beef stock for beef … etc., etc., etc..! Stir vigorously until the mixture is smooth and thickened. Add the salt and the pepper to taste and simmer for about 3-5 minutes. Strain through a fine sieve. (Makes about 1 quart)

Cranky's Tomato Sauce

5-6 tbsp. butter
2 carrots (scraped and chopped)
2 medium onions (chopped)
½ cup flour
5-6 cups tomatoes (crushed)
3-4 cups water
4 cloves garlic (crushed)
Bouquet Garni I
1 tsp. thyme (freshly chopped)
1 tsp. sea salt
2-3 tsp. sugar
1 tsp. black pepper (freshly ground)

Sauté the carrots, onions, garlic and flour in the butter until it is a light golden color and the onions are translucent in a large kettle. Add the rest of the ingredients, and simmer for enough time to get to the consistency that you desire. Strain through a fine sieve, getting as much pulp through as possible. Bring the strained liquid back to a boil and simmer for about 5-6 minutes, making sure that the sauce doesn't burn. Store the sauce in jars with a teaspoon of sherry on the top. This will keep the sauce from spoiling for a longer period of time. (Makes about 1½ quarts)

Cranky's Cream Sauce I

2 cups Cranky's Béchamel Sauce
1 cup heavy cream
1 tbsp. butter
1 tsp. lemon juice
Sea salt to taste
Black pepper to taste (freshly ground)

Place one half of the cream and all of the Béchamel sauce in a sauce pan and reduce to two cuos volume. Swirl in the rest of the cream, lemon juice and the butter, stirring constantly and season to taste. (Makes about 2 cups)

Cranky's Cream Sauce II

2 cups heavy cream
1 tbsp. flour
2 tbsp. butter (melted)
Sea salt to taste
Black pepper to taste (freshly ground)

Reduce the heavy cream in a saucepan. When the liquid is reduced, swirl in the flour and the butter quickly and simmer for 1-2 minutes. Season to taste (Makes about 1½ cups)

Cranky's Cream Sauce III

1 cup Cranky's Fish Stock
2 cup heavy cream
3-4 tbsp. flour

3-4 tbsp. butter (melted)
Sea salt to taste
Black pepper to taste (freshly ground)

Cranky's Cream Sauce IV

2 cups Cranky's Cream Sauce III
2 egg yolks (beaten

When the sauce is heated, whisk in the beaten egg yolks so that they emulsify. (Makes about 1½ cups)

Cranky's Cream Sauce V

2 cups Cranky's Cream Sauce IV
¼ heavy cream

When the cream sauce is finished, whisk in the cream and cook for 2-3 minutes and stir until smooth. (Makes about 2 cups)

Cranky's Sauce Pistou

3 cups basil leaves
1 cup parsley
¼ cup tarragon
¼ cup chervil
¼ cup chives
2 cloves garlic
2 lemons (juiced)
1-1½ cups olive oil
½ tsp. sea salt
¼ tsp. black pepper (freshly ground)

Place all of the ingredients except the olive oil in a blender and puree. Turn the blender to low and dribble in the olive oil until the consistency is that of a thin mayonnaise. (Makes about 3 cups)

Cranky's B-B-Q Sauce

After tasting many of the world's finest and famous barbecue sauces, I finally decided to publish and make known to the world, the most expensive and fantastically sensational barbecue sauce that the world has ever encountered. It is rich and hearty, strong and vibrant, thick and concentrated, and superbly flavored with over 24 ... that's right ... 24 different ingredients. All fresh and of the highest quality. Each and every one of the ingredients are needed to add a little of flavor needed to make up the gustatory taste delight that this sauce provides.

1 tbsp. curry
1 cup brandy
1 cup red wine
8 quarts tomatoes (peeled and seeded)
2 large onions (chopped)
2 cup blackstrap molasses
1 cup dark Karo syrup
1 quart Cranky's Tomato Paste
½ cup mustard (dry)
1 cup brown sugar
4 quarts water
2 tbsp. chervil (freshly chopped)
2 tbsp. tarragon (freshly chopped)
2cup parsley (freshly chopped)
2 tbsp. chives (freshly chopped)
2 tbsp. thyme (freshly chopped)
2 tbsp. basil (freshly chopped)
2 tbsp. oregano (freshly chopped)
4 cups green onions (chopped)
8-10 garlic cloves (crushed)
1 orange (peeled, seeded and finely chopped, skin included)
1 lemon orange (peeled, seeded and finely chopped, skin included)
¼ cup jalapeno (seeded and chopped)
1 tsp. hot sauce of choice
Liquid Smoke
1 block of hickory 4 X 4 X2 that has been well charred in the BBQ grill

In a 15-20 quart stock pot, place the block of charred hickory. Place a wire insert over the block to keep at the bottom of the pot. Add all of the ingredients except the smoke and the hot sauce. Bring the mixture to a rolling boil and turn to simmer. Simmer until the volume has been halved. At this time, add the last two ingredients until the sharpness fits your taste. Cool and bottle. Keep refrigerated until ready to use. (Makes about 8 quarts)

Cranky's Majestic Cocktail Sauce

This is the best cocktail sauce in the world and not your conventional cocktail sauce that is made with catsup and lemon juice and horseradish sauce. I would like to introduce you to personal recipe that I have created that will change your mind about all the cocktail sauces in the world. I truly think that this sauce will titillate your taste buds and gratify even your most sophisticated gustatory senses.

4 tbsp. red wine vinegar
2 tsp. mustard (dry)
4 egg yolks
2 tbsp celery
2 tbsp. horseradish
4 tbsp. chives
2 tbsp. parsley
2 tbsp. shallots
1 tsp. sea salt
1 tsp. black or white pepper (freshly ground)
8 ounces olive oil
4 ozs. Cognac
4 ozs. chili sauce
½ lemon (freshly squeezed)
½ lime (freshly squeezed)

Blend all of the ingredients, except the olive oil, until a smooth texture has been reached. Add the olive oil and blend till the mixture has reached an emulsion stage. (Makes about 1 quart)

Cranky's Meat Sauce

This is a rich meat sauce that will match up with anybodies. You be the judge!

4 pounds chuck (ground)
1 pound veal (ground)
2 tsp. sage (freshly chopped)
1 cup parsley (freshly chopped)
2 tbsp. oregano (freshly chopped)
2 cups green onions (freshly chopped)
2 cups green peppers (freshly chopped)
2 tsp. black pepper
4 tsp. sea salt
1½ button mushrooms (sliced)
2 large onions (chopped)
8-10 cloves garlic (minced)
4 quarts tomatoes (peeled and seeded and crushed)
1 quart Cranky's Tomato Purée
1 pint Cranky's Tomato Paste
1 quart red wine

Place everything, with the olive oil, in a large pot (15-20 quart) except the wine and the tomato products. Simmer until the onions are translucent and the meat is cooked. When they are done, add the tomatoes, tomato paste and the tomato puree and the red wine. Bring the mixture to a boil, stirring often, and turn to simmer. Simmer the sauce for about 4 hours, stirring often. When cooked and reduced, set aside and wait until the fat from the meat rises to the top. Skim the fat off the sauce and put the sauce in self-sealing jars and let cool. The sauce will keep in the refrigerator almost indefinitely. (Makes about 6 quarts)

Cranky's Tartar Sauce

2 egg yolks
1 cup olive oil
1 cup Cranky's Classic Mayonnaise
1 tsp. mustard (dry)
6-8 pimiento olives
6-8 small sweet gherkins (chopped)
2 tsp. parsley (freshly chopped)
2-3 green onions (chopped)

½ tsp tarragon (freshly chopped)
½ tsp. sea salt
1 tsp. black pepper (freshly ground)

Put everything in a blender, pulse for a few seconds and then put in a self sealing mason jar. Chill before serving. (Makes 3-4 quarts)

Cranky's Mop Sauce

1 cup olive oil
1 cup parsley (fresh chopped)
4-5 cloves garlic (minced)
3 cups tomatoes (crushed)
2 cups white wine
3 tbsp oregano (fresh chopped)
1 tsp. black pepper (freshly ground)

Put everything in a medium size kettle and simmer until the right consistency is achieved to your taste. (Makes about 2 quarts)

Cranky's Horseradish Sauce I

½ cup horseradish (freshly grated)
1 cup heavy cream (whipped)
2 tsp. lemon juice (freshly squeezed)
1 tsp. sea salt

Mix all of the ingredients together and chill. Serve with cold beef or as desired on sandwiches. Makes about 2 cups)

Cranky's Horseradish Sauce II

3 cups water
3 tbsp. flour
2 tbsp. lemon juice (freshly squeezed)
½ pound fresh horseradish (peeled and grated)
½ cup white wine vinegar
1½ cups extra virgin olive oil
Sea salt to taste

Bring the flour, water and lemon juice to a boil in a large pan. Add the horseradish and boil 2 to 3 minutes. Drain, refresh under cold water and drain again completely. Mix with the vinegar and oil and season to taste. (Makes about 1 quart)

Cranky's Beef Stock I

2 pounds beef shanks
2 pounds veal shanks
2 onions (coarsely chopped)
3-4 carrots (coarsely chopped)
8 quarts of water
4 celery stalks (chopped)
3 tsp. sea salt
1 tsp. thyme (freshly chopped)
1 Bouquet Garni IV
2 cups red wine
1 tsp. black pepper (freshly ground)

Have your butcher saw the bones in one inch lengths and place them, along with the onions and the carrots in a roasting pan with 1 quart of water. Brown the bones and meat to the desired color that you would want your stock to end up as, or the color that you would want your sauce. Put everything into a large stock pot, along with all of the other ingredients. Bring to a boil, turn to a simmer and simmer for about 10-12 hours. Replenish the water every hour up until the last two or three hours and then reduce the stock to about 3 quarts. Strain the stock through a fine sieve. Chill this in a glass bowl or in Mason jars. Let the fat seal the top to keep out bacteria and odors. You can also freeze the stock. (Makes about 3 quarts)

Cranky's Beef Stock II

2 pounds veal knuckles (split)
1 large beef knuckle (split)
4 pounds brisket (lean)
6 cleaned chicken feet
2 large onions (chopped)
2 bay leaves

2 carrots (chopped)
2-3 leeks (rinsed well and chopped)
1 large onion (porcupined with whole cloves)
10-12 whole cloves
2-4 stalks celery (chopped)
2 tsp. parsley (freshly chopped)
6 quarts water
1 tsp. sea salt

Simmer everything together for about 4 hours. Strain and store in the refrigerator. Eat the brisket. (Makes about 1½-2 quarts)

Cranky's Chicken Stock

5-6 pound stewing chicken (cut in eighths)
6-8 quarts water
2 tbsp. vegetable oil
1 large onion (quartered)
2 carrots (coarsely chopped)
4-5 celery stalks with the leaves (chopped)
2-3 cloves garlic (crushed)
2 tsp. sea salt
1 tsp. black pepper (freshly ground)
2 tsp. thyme (freshly ground)
2 tsp. parsley (freshly chopped)
2 bay leaves (crushed)
2-3 leeks (split and well rinsed)
3-4 whole cloves
2 whole allspices

In a large stock pot, place all of the vegetables and sauté them until they are soft and translucent. Add the chicken parts, including the wing tips, the neck, the giblets and even the part that goes over the fence last. Add everything else to the stock pot and simmer for at least 2 hours. Skim the top as needed. Take the chicken eighths out of the pot and cool. Pick off the meat for a later recipe. (chicken salad or to make a chicken forcemeat) Chop the bones and the skin and everything other than the chicken meat and return to the put. Add some water and simmer for another 6-8 hours, adding water the first 6 hours as needed. When finished, strain the mixture through a fine sieve and place in Mason jars. Leave the fat … it will come to the top and seal the stock and help preserve, as well as, keeping refrigerator odors out of the stock. (Makes about 2 quarts)

Susie's Veal Stock I

4 pounds veal knuckles (chopped up)
½ cup olive oil
6-7 quarts water
1 large onion (coarsely chopped)
3-4 cloves
2 carrots (chopped)
3-4 leeks (rinsed and chopped)
3-4 celery stalks
1 Bouquet Garni II
1 tsp. sea salt
½ tsp. black pepper (freshly ground)
2 tsp. thyme (freshly chopped)
2 pounds of chicken giblets (with livers)

In a large stock pot, braise the bones in olive oil. Add the water and all of the rest of the ingredients except the chicken giblets. Simmer for about 4-5 hours, skimming as needed. This is a must. Chop the giblets and add to the pot with 3-4 quarts of water. Simmer for another 3-4 hours. Strain the liquid through a fine sieve, making sure that you get as much of the liquid out of the solids that you can. Place in Mason jars and allow the fat to seal the stock. It will come to the top and seal the stock and help preserve, as well as, keeping refrigerator odors out of the stock. (Makes about 2-3 quarts)

Cranky's Veal Stock II

3-4 pounds veal knuckles (chopped up
1½ pounds veal (cubed) 6-7 quarts water
1 tsp. sea salt
1 tsp. whole peppercorns (crushed)
1 large onion (coarsely chopped)
3-4 whole cloves

Bouquet Garni II

Place all of the ingredients into a stock pot and simmer for 6-8 hours. Skim the scum off the top as needed and add water as needed up to the last 2 hour. Strain and store in Mason jars and allow the fat seal the stock. It will come to the top and seal the stock and help preserve, as well as, keeping refrigerator odors out of the stock. (Makes about 1½ quarts)

Cranky's Fish Stock

This recipe makes the best fish stock in the world, and I defy any cook or chef to make a better one! I always try to use salt water fish for salt water fare recipes and fresh water fish for fresh water fare recipes.

2 pounds of fish head, bones and fins (chopped)
¼ cup butter
2 cups onions (chopped)
2 cups parsley (freshly chopped)
1 lemon (chopped)
1 tsp. sea salt
3-4 quarts water
1 quart white wine
1 tsp. white pepper (freshly ground)
2 tsp. chervil (freshly chopped)
1 tsp. chives (freshly snipped)

For either a freshwater or a saltwater stock … it helps to throw in some skate bones, it will help to enrich the stock. I also like to use only white flesh fish … they have less oil and less of an aftertaste. Sauté the fish parts in the butter along with the onions and the rest of the ingredients, except the wine. Do not brown the onions … they might cause another kind of an aftertaste. When the items have been sautéed, place all of the items, including the water and wine in a large kettle and simmer for about 4-5 hours. Strain the stock into pint containers and freeze the stock. (Makes about 1½ quarts)

Cranky's Clam Stock

2-3 cherrystones (scrubbed)

6-7 cups water
1 tbsp. olive oil
4 shallots (coarsely chopped)
3-4 tbsp parsley (freshly chopped)

Scrub the clams and place them in a large kettle, sprinkle with olive oil. Add the water and the rest of the ingredients. Simmer until the clams open. Remove the clams from the kettle and take the clams out of the shells. Freeze the steamed clams for your next chowder day. Strain the broth through a fine sieve lined with very fine cheesecloth. This can be and should be frozen if not used immediately. (Makes about 1-2 quarts)

Cranky's Shrimp Stock

5-10 pounds of raw shrimp (heads and shells on)
1 medium onion stuck with whole cloves
2-3 slices of lemon
½ bay leaf
½ tsp. parsley (freshly chopped)
4-5 stalks celery (chopped)
4 quarts water

Cook the shrimp as always, removing them from the heat when the just curl. Allow to cool. Peel the shrimp and save the heads, the tails and the shells. Freeze the peeled shrimp for your next cocktail party. Chop the shells, tail and head and return to the pot. Simmer for about 8 hours so that the fat in the heads comes out completely. If you have any spare fish heads or fish bones in the freezer ... throw them it as well ... it will only make for a better and richer stock. Reduce the stock to about 2 quarts. Strain and freeze the stock for later use. Use this stock as directed. (Makes about 2 quarts)

Cranky's Lobster Stock

Shells 8-10 one and half pound lobsters
2 cups white wine
½ cup brandy
2 tbsp. butter
¼ cup celery (chopped)

¼ cup carrot (chopped)
1 onion (chopped)
1 leek (chopped and rinsed)
2 garlic cloves (minced)
1 tbsp. parsley (freshly chopped)
2 tbsp Cranky's Tomato Paste
1 tomato (chopped)
1 tbsp. thyme (freshly chopped)
3 quarts water

Roast the lobster shells for 10 minutes at 325 degrees. Put the shells into a stock pot and add all of the rest of the ingredients after you have sautéed the vegetables. Simmer until the liquid is reduced by half. Strain the liquid into plastic containers and freeze for future use. (Makes about 5-6 cups)

Cranky's Vegetable Stock

2 medium onions (peeled)
4 stalks celery
2 green onions
2 carrots (scraped)
1 large potato (peeled)
1-2 turnips (peeled)
1 pound spinach (washed and rinsed)
½ cup parsley (chopped)

Chop all of the ingredients and place in a food processor. Blend and bring the mixture to a boil in a soup kettle with 4 quarts of water. Cover and simmer for 1-2 hours. Uncover and reduce to half volume. Strain through a fine sieve and freeze for later use. (Makes about 1 quart of Vegetable stock)

Cranky's Court Bouillon

1 quart water
1 medium onion stuck with 4-5 cloves
1-2 slices of onion
½ bay leaf
½ tsp. parsley (freshly chopped)
½ stalk celery with leaves (chopped)

1 tsp. sea salt

Simmer all of the ingredients for 15-20 minutes before adding the fish that you wish to poach. Remember that you have to have enough liquid to cover the fish that you are going to poach. Adjust the recipe accordingly to fit the fish.

Cranky's White Wine Court Bouillon for Fish

Add to the Court Bouillon recipe the following items:

1 quart dry white wine
2 carrots (scrapped and chopped)
1 medium onion (chopped)
10-12 black peppercorns
Bouquet Garni III

Simmer for 30 minutes before introducing the fish.

Cranky's Maitre D'Hotel Butter

1 pound of butter
3-4 tbsp. lemon juice (freshly squeezed)
5-6 tbsp. parsley (freshly chopped)
1 tsp. sea salt
1 tsp. black pepper (freshly ground)

Melt the butter and add the lemon juice, parsley, salt and pepper. This can be served melted or chilled and solid and served on top of steaks and chops in a lump as a garnish.

Cranky's Clarified Butter

2-3 pounds butter

Place the butter in a double boiler and cook on a low simmer until the white portions, the whey and the casein, have settled to the bottom of the pot. Skim off the foam on the top and pour the butter oil through some cheesecloth, being careful not to allow the casein or whey to touch the cheesecloth. Store in the refrigerator.

Cranky's Lobster Butter à la Maison

When I broil lobsters, after I split them, I take out the tomalley and the coral (liver and roe) and save it in order to make a rich lobster butter. This is a recipe that I have never found anywhere in any other cookbook and I am sure that you will enjoy its tangy taste.

Roe and liver from 3-4 female lobsters
2 pounds of butter
½ tbsp parsley (freshly minced)
1 tsp. green onion (minced)
½ tsp. sea salt
¼ tsp. white pepper (freshly ground)
1-2 dashes Tabasco sauce
1 tsp. lemon juice (freshly squeezed)
1-2 quarts of water

Place the butter and one half of the water in the top of a double boiler and let the butter melt. Blend all of the rest of the ingredients in a food blender and blend for about 20-30 seconds. Pour the rest of the hot water into the blender and blend for about 5 seconds. Pour this mixture into the top of the double boiler and mix thoroughly. Take off the heat and chill in the refrigerator until the butter hardens. Pack and seal the hardened butter in an earthenware crock, seal the crock and refrigerate. Unsealed, it will spoil rather quickly.

Cranky's Green Butter

12 spinach leaves
12 watercress leaves
1 tbsp. parsley (freshly minced)
1 tbsp tarragon (freshly minced)
1 tsp. chervil (freshly minced)
1 pound of butter (melted)

Poach the spinach, parsley, tarragon, chervil and the watercress leaves in boiling water for 3-4 minutes. Strain and rinse in cold water. Allow the mixture to dry. Force the mixture through a fine strainer along with the melted butter. Store in the same manner … in an covered earthenware crock.

Cranky's Parsley Butter

Follow the same procedure for Cranky's Green Butter but use only one tablespoon of fresh minced parsley for every tablespoon of butter. If using immediately, it is not necessary to poach the parsley. If storing, follow the same instructions.

Cranky's Sorrel Butter Chiffonade

5-6 tbsp. sorrel leaves (cut into strips
½ pound butter

Place the sorrel strips and the butter in a thick saucepan and cook slowly until the sorrel liquid evaporates. Put in a small plastic container and let the butter solidify.

Cranky's Chipotle Butter

6 tbsp. butter (softened)
1 or 2 chipotle chilies (chopped fine)
½ tsp. sea salt
1 tsp. lime juice (freshly squeezed)

Blend all of the ingredients. Place in a plastic container and store, covered, in the refrigerator. (Makes about ½ cup)

Cranky's Seafood Seasoning Salt

2 tbsp. sea salt
2 tbsp. black pepper (ground)
2 tbsp. onion salt
2 tbsp. garlic salt
2 tbsp. sugar
2 tbsp. celery salt

2 tbsp. chervil (dried)
2 tbsp. dill weed (dried)
2 tbsp. lemon zest (dried)

Mix all of these items together in a stainless steel bowl thoroughly and place all of it in large salt shaker or a large re-usable spice shaker. (Makes about 1 cup)

Cranky's Fines Herbes

This mixture can be used in hundreds of recipes or just left on the dinner table and used like a seasoning salt on hamburgers, spaghetti, soups and any number of broiled or roasted meat, steaks, chops, broiled chicken, salads, you name it.

1 bunch of fresh parsley
1 bunch of fresh chervil
1 bunch of fresh tarragon
1 bunch of fresh sweet basil
1 bunch of fresh thyme
1 bunch of fresh dill
1 bunch of fresh oregano
1 bunch of fresh rosemary
1 bunch of fresh sage
1 bunch of fresh watercress
1 bunch of fresh chives
4 tbsp. celery salt
4 tbsp. onion salt
4 tbsp. garlic salt
4 tbsp. paprika

Try to start with the same size bunches. Wash all of the fresh items and shake as dry as possible. Chop all of the fresh items coarsely and place them in a large wooden salad bowl. Toss them frequently until they are dried, not completely because they lose their power. Rub he dried herbs through a fine colander into a large bowl. Add the rest of the ingredients and mix everything well together. Put this mixture into mason jars that have the covers and the rings … punch a few holes in the tops from the outside and store in your spice cabinet. Use this spice and herb mixture when desired or needed. I leave one on the dinner table for salads.

Cranky's Bouquet Garni I

A bouquet garni is an assortment of herbs and spices that are tied together in a cheesecloth bag and put in cooking pots for the purpose of flavor, but meant to be removed from the pot at some time or other during the cooking process. The bag makes this an easy chore. The most common bouquet garni consists of the following:

1-6 inch square of cheesecloth
1 tbsp. parsley
1 tsp. thyme
1 bay leaf
1 tsp. celery seed

Cranky's Bouquet Garni II

1-6 inch square of cheesecloth
1 tbsp. parsley
1 tsp. thyme
1 bay leaf
1 tsp. celery seed
6 juniper berries

Cranky's Bouquet Garni III

1-6 inch square of cheesecloth
2 tbsp. parsley
½ tsp. thyme
2 bay leaves
2-4 cloves

Cranky's Bouquet Garni IV

1-6 inch square of cheesecloth
3 tbsp. parsley
½ tsp. thyme
1 bay leaf

Cranky's Bouquet Garni V

6 inch square of cheesecloth
1-tsp. fennel
1 tsp. chives
1 tsp. marjoram
1 tsp. tarragon
1 bay leaf

Cranky's Bouquet Garni VI

6 inch square of cheesecloth
6-8 cloves
3-4 bay leaves
10-12 black peppercorns
1-2 allspice

Cranky's Picada

2 loaves of white bread (crust removed)
4 cups olive oil
4 cups almonds (blanched)
4 ancho chilies (dried poblanos)
4 cups boiling water
4 jalapeno chilies (seeded and minced)
1 tsp. sea salt
20-30 garlic cloves (chopped)

Slice the bread and sauté all of the slices in the olive oil. Toast the almonds until they are a pale brown. Soak the ancho chilies in boiling water for 20 minutes. Remove the anchos, cut them in half and remove all of the seeds. Strain the olive oil into a food processor and all of the other ingredients. Process for about one minute, add the bread and process until a smooth paste is accomplished. (Makes about 1½ quarts)

Cranky's Duxelles

2 pounds button mushrooms
1 cup onion (chopped)

½ cup shallots (chopped)
½ cup butter
2 tbsp. olive oil
¼ tsp. sea salt
¼ tsp. black pepper (freshly ground)

Place the mushrooms in a clean, fine-meshed towel and squeeze the moisture out of them. Saute the mushrooms, onions and shallots in the butter and the olive oil until all of the moisture has evaporated. Did the salt and pepper to taste. (Makes about 2½ cups)

Cranky's Glace de Viande

2 quarts Cranky's Veal Stock

Reduce the veal stock with fat removed from the top of the broth. Reduce the stock until it is syrupy. Transfer this glace de viande to a freezer container and keep it in the freezer indefinitely. When needed, dip a spoon in boiling water and ladle out the desired amount of the mixture. (Makes about 1½ cups)

Cranky's Coconut Cream

2-3 coconuts
2-3 cups milk

Crack the coconuts over a stainless steel bowl. Save the coconut milk and the meat with all of the brown parts removed and put all in a food processor and process until smooth. Scald the milk and place everything into the top of a double boiler. Cook over simmering water for about 1-1½ hours. Chill thoroughly and lift the coconut cream from the surface. (Makes about 3 cups)

Cranky's Crème Fraîche

1 pint heavy cream
½ pint sour cream

Pour the sour cream into a heavy saucepan and stir in the heavy cream. Heat to warm to start bacterial action but do not exceed 90 degrees. The use of a candy thermometer can be helpful at this point. Set out, partially covered at room temperature or until it has thickened naturally. Stir and store in the refrigerator. This will last as long as sour cream. (Makes about 1½ cups)

Cranky's Tomato Paste

6-8 pounds ripe tomatoes

Seed and peel and chop the tomatoes and rub them through a colander. Cook the tomatoes in a saucepan for about 15-20 minutes on simmer. Strain this mixture, when cool, through a fine piece of cheesecloth to eliminate the water. The remaining pulp is tomato paste.

Cranky's Tomato Purée

12 large tomatoes
1 tsp. caraway seeds
½ cup butter
2 onions (chopped)
1 cup celery (chopped)
4 tbsp. parsley
1 tsp. lemon juice (freshly squeezed)

Chop the tomatoes, peels, seeds and all in a large kettle. Sauté the remaining ingredients and add to the kettle. Simmer for about 1½-2 hours. Squeeze the mixture through a fine sieve, add the lemon juice and stir. Return the mixture to the kettle and reduce to a pasty texture. (Makes about 1½ quarts)

Cranky's Roux

½ pound butter
2 cups flour

Melt the butter in an iron skillet and stir in the flour until blended. Place the skillet on the heat; whisk constantly for as long as necessary or until the proper color is obtained. Remove and let stand for 2-3 hours before use. Generally, roux is made with a mixture of flour and butter or oil on a 50-50 basis. The color of the roux will determine the color of your sauce and visa versa. The more you cook the roux … the darker the sauce.

Cranky's Blonde Roux

Cook the roux for 2-3 minutes longer than regular roux.

Cranky's Golden Roux

Cook the roux for 4-6 minutes longer than regular roux.

Cranky's Brown Roux

Cook the roux for 7-9 minutes longer than regular roux.

Cranky's Black Roux

Cook the roux for 10-12 minutes longer than regular roux.

Cranky's Crab Boil Mixture

4 ozs. Cranky's Pickling Spice
2 cups sea salt
½ cup cayenne pepper
½ cup onion powder
¼ cup garlic powder
¼ cup grated lemon peel

Mix all of the ingredients together. Use 1 cup for every dozen crabs and 4 quarts of water.

Cranky's Salsa Verde

2 slices of white bread
½ cup red wine vinegar
1 large bunch of Italian parsley
2 anchovies
1-2 garlic cloves
1 hard boiled egg
1 tsp. capers
1 cup extra-virgin olive oil
Sea salt and black pepper to taste

Soak the bread in the vinegar and squeeze out the liquid. Blend all of the ingredients, except the olive oil, until smooth buy not liquefied. Transfer to a steel or glass bowl and dribble in the olive oil, whisking until the sauce emulsifies. (Makes about 1 quart)

Cranky's Salsa Rosa

3 pounds or ripe tomatoes (seeded and chopped finely)
1 yellow sweet pepper (seeded and chopped)
1 red sweet pepper (seeded and chopped)
1 onion (chopped)
2 tsp. hot chili pepper (minced)
¼ cup sugar
¼ cup white wine vinegar
½ cup extra-virgin olive oil
Sea salt to taste
Black pepper to taste (freshly ground)

In a heavy-based saucepan, combine all of the ingredients except the vinegar and the olive oil. And simmer over very low heat until everything is soft and the texture of marmalade. This takes about an hour … maybe less. Puree the mixture, return it to the pan and stir in the vinegar and season to taste. Cook for 10 minutes more or until the mixture is very thick. Cool. Just before serving, whisk in enough olive oil to loosen the texture and enrich the flavor of the sauce. (Makes about 1 quart)

Cranky's Red Mayonnaise

1 large boiled beet
½ tsp. red wine vinegar
1 quart Cranky's Classic Mayonnaise

Puree a boiled beet with the vinegar and fold into the mayonnaise. (Makes just over a quart)

Cranky's Green Mayonnaise

4 cups Cranky's Classic Mayonnaise
2 tbsp tarragon (fresh)

2 tbsl. chives (freshly snipped)
2 tbsp. parsley (freshly chopped)
2 tsp. chervil (freshly chopped)
2 tsp. dill (freshly chopped)

Blend all of the ingredients until the proper is achieved. Let chill for 3-4 hours before serving. (makes about 1 quart)

Cranky's Classic Mayonnaise

I like to use different kinds of oil, when available, such as sunflower, groundnut or corn oil. It changes the flavor of the mayonnaise in a remarkable manner. Lemon juice is a must for white mayonnaise in addition to the taste.

6-12 egg yolks
6 cups olive oil (approximately)
Tarragon vinegar to taste
Lemon juice to taste
Sea salt to taste
White pepper to taste (freshly ground)

Place everything in a blender on low and drizzle the olive oil or oil f your choice into the blender very slowly. Flavor the mayonnaise to taste with the tarragon vinegar. (Makes about 2 quarts)

Cranky's Basic Pie Crust

3 cups flour
½ tsp. sea salt
3 egg yolks
¾ cups butter (softened)
1 tbsp. olive oil
1 cup cold water

Sift the flour and salt together into a large bowl. Make a little volcano in the flour mixture and place the egg yolks, softened butter and olive oil in the well. Blend the ingredients in the well to a smooth paste with your fingers. Gradually add the flour to the paste while adding the cold water in small increments. This should make a dough that holds its shape and doesn't stick to the sides of the bowl or the rolling board. Cover with a light and damp cloth for about 1 hour before rolling. (Makes both bottom and top crusts for one pie)

Cranky's Fig and Fruit Fritter Batter

1 cup white wine
1½ cup flour (sifted)
2 eggs
½ tsp. sea salt
2 egg whites
½ cup figs (finely chopped)

Beat the flour and eggs until the mixture is smooth. Fold in the chopped figs and let set for 30-40 minutes. Add the saly to the egg whites and beat until stiff. Fold into the batter and spoon the batter into the hot oil and fry until golden brown.

Cranky's Rainbow Trout Stuffing

2 tbsp. onions (chopped)
4 large mushrooms of choice
½ cup almonds (blanched and chopped)
3-4 tbsp. butter
1 tsp. poultry seasoning
½ pound shrimp meat
½ pound crab meat
2 tbsp. parsley (freshly chopped)
1 cup dry white wine
2-3 tbsp. Parmesan cheese (freshly grated)
½ sea salt
1 tsp. black pepper (freshly ground)

Sauté the vegetables in the butter until the onions are translucent. Add the rest of the ingredients, mix well and cook the mixture for about 2 minutes. Let cool. (Enough for about 8 trout)

Cranky's Hot Like Hell Horseradish

2 large horseradish roots

1 tsp. sea salt
1 tsp. lemon juice (freshly squeezed)
2 tsp. white wine vinegar

Peel the chilled horseradish and cut into small pieces. Place the pieces in a food processor along with the salt and the lemon juice and the white wine vinegar. Processor the horseradish until the proper consistency. Chill the horseradish immediately. (Makes 2-3 cups)

Hot Like Hell Mustard

1 pound dry Coleman's mustard
1 pound granulated sugar
1-2 bottles lager beer or stout
1 tsp. cayenne pepper (freshly ground)
½ tsp. Tabasco sauce

Mix all of the ingredients together and whisk until completely smooth. Allow to stand in the open overnight. If you place it in a covered crock immediately and put it in the refrigerator, you will be scraping the crock top and the mustard off the walls of the refrigerator within a day or two. The next day, beat well and place in an earthenware crock. Refrigerate. Stir well before serving … the longer it is in the crock or crocks … the stronger it will get. (Makes about 1-1½ quarts)

White Wine Sauce I, II or III

Just add a dry white wine to the Cream Sauce I, II and III sauces in this cookbook.

Cranky's Saffron Rice

3 cups white rice (raw and untreated)
6-8 cups water
4-5 tbsp. butter
1 tsp. sea salt
2 pinches of saffron

Bring the rice and the water to a boil in a saucepan. Add the salt, butter and the saffron. Stir, cover and simmer for 15 minutes or until all of the liquid has been absorbed. Lift the rice from the bottom. Do not stir the rice or it will come out like glue. When the liquid has been absorbed, remove from the heat and set aside, still covered for another 10 minutes. Fluff the rice with a fork just before serving and correct the seasoning. (Serves 8)

Cranky's Wild Rice

1 cup uncooked wild rice
4 tbsp. butter
2 tsp. sea salt
2-3 cups water

Wash the rice in cold water, strain and place the rice in a covered double boiler with the water, butter and the salt. Cook for about an hour or until fluffy and dry. (Makes about 3 cups)

Cranky's Parsley Potatoes

24 small new potatoes (peeled)
1 cup melted butter
1 tsp. sea salt
1 cup parsley (freshly chopped)

Boil the potatoes and drain well. Heat the butter but do not let it burn. Add the parsley and the salt and pour over the potatoes. Toss and serve.

Cranky's Cauliflower Gratinée

5-6 cups cauliflower flowers
1-1½ cups butter (melted)
½ cup parsley (freshly chopped)
1-1½ cups Parmesan cheese (freshly grated)

Stem the cauliflower until firm but tender. Drain, add the butter and the parsley and the cheese and toss in an ovenware dish and brown lightly under the broiler. (Serves 8)

Cranky's Brussels Sprouts Gratinée

2-3 pounds Brussels sprouts (trimmed)
6 tbsp. melted butter
½ cup Parmesan cheese (freshly grated)
1 tbsp. parsley (freshly chopped)

Cook the sprouts in lightly salted water. Drain, place in a heated serving bowl and toss with the parsley and the cheese and the melted butter. (Serves 8)

Cranky's Glazed Carrots

2 pounds of baby carrots (peeled)
½ cup butter (melted)
½ cup brown sugar

Boil the carrots until tender. Drain and transfer to a skillet along with the butter and the brown sugar. Sauté the carrots or bake the carrots until the butter and the brown sugar have almost caramelized. (Serves 8)

Cranky's Pistachio Crust

6 ozs. corn chips (crushed)
1½ cups pistachio nuts (shelled)
¼ cup Dijon mustard
1 cup peanut oil
2 tbsp. chili powder
1 tbsp. rosemary (freshly chopped)
¼ tsp. sea salt

Process the chips and the nuts in a processor until coarse and not pasty. Combine the rest of the ingredients and use as needed. (Makes about 1 quart)

Bibliography

A list of research resources, books, published articles, restaurateurs, chefs and friends.

A Treasury of Great Recipes by Mary & Vincent Price 1965
Amy Vanderbilt's Complete Cookbook 1961
Antoinette Pope School Cookbook by Antoinette and Francois Pope 1948
Antoinette Pope School Cookbook by Antoinette and Francois Pope 1953
Bouquet of France by Samuel Chamberlain 1952
British Bouquet by Samuel Chamberlain 1963
Clifford A. Wright Website
Cooking with the Firehouse Chef 2003
Encyclopedia Britannica 2004
Gourmet Cookbook 1950
Gourmet Cookbook Volume II 1957
Gourmet Soup Cookbook 1995
Gourmet's Basic French Cookbook 1961
Gourmet's Best Desserts 1987
Gourmet's Menu Cookbook
Gourmet's Old Vienna Cookbook 1959
L'Art de Cuisine by Toulouse-Lautrec & Maurice Joyant 1964 (English Version)
L'Art de Cuisine by Toulouse-Lautrec & Maurice Joyant 1964 (French Version)
L'Art de Cuisine by Toulouse-Lautrec & Maurice Joyant 1964 (Italian Version)
Larousse Gastronomique 1938
Larousse Gastronomique 1961
Larousse Gastronomique 2001

Larousse Gastronomique 2003
Mastering the Art of French Cooking by Julia Child, Simone Beck & Louisette Bertholle 1961
New York Times Cookbook by Craig Claybourne 1966
Recipes of All Nations by Countess Morphy 1935
Susie's Cookbook and Kitchen Helper 1996
The Best of Gourmet 1996
The Best of Gourmet 1997
The Best of Gourmet 1998
The Encyclopedia of Fish Cookery by A. J. McClane & Arie deZanger 1977
The Great American Cookbook 1994
The Harry Caray's Restaurant Cookbook 2003
The New Antoinette Pope School Cookbook by Antoinette & Francois Pope 1961
The New Antoinette Pope School Cookbook by Antoinette Pope 1973
The Romagnolis' Italian Fish Cookbook
The French Chef Cookbook by Julia Child 1961

Restaurants, Cocktail Lounges, Saloons and Parties that Helped to Make These Cookbooks Possible

"21" Club, New York City, New York
Abacus, Chicago, Illinois
Acme Oyster House, New Orleans, Louisiana
Adolphus Hotel, Dallas, Texas
Aerhotel Baglioni, Florence, Italy
Aft Deck Oyster Bar, New Orleans, Louisiana
Air France First Class, Chicago, Illinois
Aisley Hotel, Atlanta, Georgia
Al Ain Inter-Continental Hotel, Abu Dhabi, U. A. E.
Ala Mere Catherine, Paris, France
Alameda Plaza, Kansas City, Missouri
Alfie's, Chicago, Illinois
Algonquin Hotel, New York City, New York
Alitalia, Rome, Italy
Allard, Paris, France
Allendale's Bar and Grill, Allendale, New Jersey
Alois Dallmayr, Munich, Germany
Am Franziskanerplatz, Vienna, Austria
Ambassador's East, Chicago, Illinois
Ambria. Chicao, Illinois
Amstel Hotel, Amsterdam, Holland
Amtrac Railways, Chicago, Illinois
Amtrak Dining Car Selections, Chicago, Illinois
Anatoel Hotel, Dallas Texas
Anderson's Restaurant, Maywood, Illinois
Andrew Jackson, New Orleans, Louisiana
Anfa Hotel, Casablanca, Western French Morocco
Angelo's Fisherman's Wharf, Houston, Texas
Ann Sather, Chicago, Illinois
Annabelle's, London, England
Annabelle's Fish Market, Chicago, Illinois
Ansley Hotel, Atlanta, Georgia
Anthony's, St Louis, Missouri

Antigva Casa Sobrino de Botin, Madrid, Spain
Antoine's, New Orleans, Louisiana
Anything Goes, New Orleans, Louisiana
Ardsheal House, Argyllshire, Scotland
Arizona Biltmore, Phoenix, Arizona
Ashiya, Kyoto, Japan
Atlanta Biltmore Hotel, Atlanta, Georgia
Atlantic Restaurant, Chicago, Illinois
Auberge St Eustache, Paris, France
August Moon, Chicago, Illinois
Austin Koo's Mandarin, Chicago, Illinois
Azuma Japanese Restaurant, Chicago, Illinois
Antoine's ... New Orleans ... USA
Bacino's Pizza, Chicago, Illinois
Bahama House, Paradise Island, Bahamas
Bal du Moulin Rouge, Paris, France
Bali, Amsterdam, Holland
Balmoral Beach, Nassau, Bahamas
Banff Springs Hotel, Banff, Alberta, Canada
Barney's, Chicago, Illinois
Baumaniere, Les Baux, France
Beat Kitchen, Chicago, Illinois
Beau Sejour, Long Island, New York
Beaumont, Chicago, Illinois
Beggar's Serf, Chicago, Illinois
Begue's Restaurant, New Orleans, Louisiana
Belle Angeline Riverboat, St Louis, Missouri
Belle Terrase, Copenhagen, Denmark
Bellvue-Stratford Hotel, Philadelphia, Pennsylvania
Bengal Lancers, Chicago, Illinois
Benihana East, New York City, New York
Beau Sejour ... Long Island ... USA
Belle Terrasse ... Copenhagen ... Denmark
Ben's, Calgary, Alberta Canada
Beques, New Orleans, Louisiana
Berghoff's Men's Bar, Chicago, Illinois
Bertita's Bar, Taxco, Mexico
Bessborough Hotel, Saskatoon, Saskatchuwan
Beverly Hills Hotel, Beverly Hills, California
Beverly Hilton, Los Angeles, California
Biltmore Hotel, Los Angeles, California
Bistrot de Paris, Paris, France
Blue Lagoon, Chicago, Illinois
Blue Point Chowder House, Chicago, Illinois
Blues Alley, New Orleans, Louisiana
Boca Raton Hotel and Club, Boca Raton, Florida
Boccaccio's, Chicago, Illinois
Bon Ton Café, New Orleans, Louisiana
Bonaventure Hotel and Spa, Ft Lauderdale, Florida
Bootlegger's, Chicago, Illinois
Boston Sea Party, Lincolnshire, Illinois

Boulestin, London, England
Brandy House, San Francisco, California
Brassary, Chicago, Illinois
Breakfast Nook-Marriott Long Wharf, Boston, Massachusetts
Brennan's, New Orleans, Louisiana
Briar Hall Golf and Country Cob, Briarcliff, New York
Bristol Seafood Grill, Oakbrook, Illinois
British Airways, London, England
Broussard's, New Orleans, Louisiana
Bucket of Blood Club, Chicago, Illinois
Budd Javid's Pizza, Chicago, Illinois
Bull and Bear Bar-Waldorf Hotel, New York City, New York
Bundesbahn, Munich, Germany
Burhop's, Chicago, Illinois
Bush Garden, Portland, Oregon
Byfield's, Chicago, Illinois
Caesar's Hotel, Tijuana, Mexico
Caesar's Palace, Las Vegas, Nevada
Café des Artistes, Key West, Florida
Café Figaro, Chicago, Illinois
Café Kenessey Restaurant, Chicago, Illinois
Café Louis IX, Hull, Ontario Canada
Café Martinique, Paradise Island, Bahamas
Café Pontchartrain, New Orleans, Louisiana
Café Raul's, Chicago, Illinois
Café Roma, New Orleans, Louisiana
Café Royal-Royal Orleans, New Orleans, Louisiana
Café Tu Tu Tango, Buckhead, Georgia
Café Tu Tu Tango, Orlando, Florida
Cajun Cabin, New Orleans, Louisiana
Calo Italian Cuisine, Chicago, Illinois
Camelback Inn, Phoenix, Arizona
Campfire Club of America, Chappaqua, NewYork
Caneel Bay, Paradise Island, Bahamas
Captain's Bar, Mandarin Hotel, Kowloon, Hong Kong
Caribbean Room, Montego Bay, Jamaican
Caribe Hilton Hotel, San Juan, Puerto Rice
Carre de Veau a la Duxelles, Amsterdam, Holland
Cartagena, Hotel Hilton, Catagena, Columbia
Carver's Table-Pheasant Run, St Charles, Illinois
Casa Marina Marriott, Key West, Florida
Casanova Grill Bar, Naples, Italy
Casey's Shortstop, Chicago, Illinois
Casina Valadier, Rome, Italy
Cathay Mandarin Restaurant, Elmwood Park, Illinois
Cavalieri Hiltom International, Rome, Italy
Cazadores, Guadalajara, Mexico

Cedar Rapids Town House Motor, Cedar Rapids, Iowa
Centro Ristorante, Chicago, Illinois
Champagne Room-Prince de Galles, Paris, France
Chapulin, Chicago, Illinois
Boulestin ... London ... England
Bush Garden ... Portland ... USA
Captain Hook's Pirate Cove ... Chicago ... USA
Casina Valadier ... Rome ... Italy
Charley's, Boston, Massachusetts
Charlie's Café Exceptionale, Minneapolis, Minnesota
Chateau Frontenac, Quebec City, Quebec, Canada
Chateau Laurier, Ottowa, Ontario, Canada
Chavez Ravine, Los Angeles, California
Cheers/Bull & Finch Pub, Boston, Massachusetts
Chef Alberto's, Chicago, Illinois
Chen's Small Eating Place, Cambridge, Massachusetts
Chestnut Street Grill, Chicago, Illinois
Chicago Palm Restaurant, Chicago, Illinois
Chicago Pizza & Oven Grinder, Chicago, Illinois
China Airlines, Peking, China
China Inn Restaurant, Washington, DC
China Spice, Chicago, Illinois
Chiquini's, Chicago, Illinois
Chon y Chano, Chicago, Illinois
Chavez Ravine ... Los Angeles ... USA
Club Gene & Georgetti, Chicago, Illinois
Cock n' Bull Restaurant, Los Angeles, California
College Inn-Hotel Sherman, Chicago, Illinois
Colonnade Hotel, Boston, Massachusetts
Conrad Hilton Hotel, Chicago, Illinois
Convito Italiano, Chicago, Illinois
Convito Italiano, Winnetka, Illinois
Coral Harbor Restaurant, Nassau, Bahamas
Coral Lounge, Gilman, Illinois
Coralla, Rome, Italy
Counselor's Row, Chicago, Illinois
Country Flame, New Orleans, Louisiana
Coureurs de Bois, Kansas City, Missouri
Court of Two Sisters, New Orleans, Louisiana
Courtyard Café, Toronto, Ontario Canada
Courtyard Café-Marriott, New Orleans, Louisiana
Crown Point Hotel, Tobago, Trinidad
Cubbie Bear Lounge, Chicago, Illinois
Cy's Crab House, Chicago, Illinois
D.B. Kaplan's, Chicago, Illinois
D'Augostino's, Chicago, Illinois
Dave & Buster's, Atlanta, Georgia
Dave & Buster's, Chicago, Illinois

Dave & Buster's, Dallas, Texas
Dave & Buster's, Houston, Texas
Dave & Buster's, Philadelphia, Pennsylvania
Dearborn Street Oyster Bar, Chicago, Illinois
Delmonico's, New York City, New York
Denny's, Madison, Wisconsin
Desire, New Orleans, Louisiana
Diana's Grocery, Chicago, Illinois
Diana's, Chicago, Illinois
Diana's Grocery & Restaurant, Chicago, Illinois
Dikker en Thijs, Amsterdam, Holland
Dinner at the Fritz, Evanston, Illinois
Dockside at Malden, Malden, Massachusetts
Dockside Boston's, Boston, Massachusetts
Domeliner, Los Angeles, California
Don Roth's Blackhawk, Chicago, Illinois
Don the Beachcomber's, Honolulu, Hawaii
Don's Fishmarket, Chicago, Illinois
Dorado Beach Hotel, Dorado Beach, Puerto Rico
Dorinne Dunbar's, New Orleans, Louisiana
Dos Hermanos Cantina, Chicago, Illinois
Dragon Inn, Glenwood, Illinois
Drake Hotel, Chicago, Illinois
Drake University Club, Des Moines, Iowa
Du Midi, New York City, New York
Dumpling Inn, London, England
Durgin-Park, Boston, Massachusetts
East River Yacht Club, New York City, New York
East Winds Inn, Castries, St. Lucia
Eat a Pita, Chicago, Illinois
Eddie Rockets, Chicago, Illinois
Edgewater Hotel, Chicago, Illinois
Dikker and Thijs ... Amsterdam ... Holland
Dorado Beach Hotel ... Puerto Rico ... USA
Du Midi ... New York City ... USA
Durgin-Park ... Boston ... USA
Edgewater Hotel, Chicago, Illinois
El Jardin, Chicago, Illinois
El Panama Hotel, Panama City, Panama
Elias Brothers, Warren, Michigan
Ember's Steak House, New Orleans, Louisiana
Emeril's, New Orleans, Louisiana
Empress of China Restaurant, San Francisco, California
Ernie's, San Francisco, California
Eugene's, Chicago, Illinois
Europaisher Hof, Frankfort, Germany
Fairfield Inn, Lincolnshire, Illinois
Fairmont Hotel, San Francisco, California
Edgewater Hotel, Honolulu, Hawaii
Edwardo's Pizzeria, Chicago, Illinois
Ernie's ... San Francisco ... USA
Famous Deli & Pub, Evanston, Illinois

Far East Restaurant, Chicago, Illinois
Father and Son Pizzeria, Chicago, Illinois
Field's Steak & Stein, Wisconsin Dells, Wisconsin
Fiesta Mexicana, Chicago, Illinois
Fingers Restaurant, Calgary, Alberta Canada
Finley's, Chicago, Illinois
Fireplace Inn, Chicago, Illinois
Five O'Clock Lounge, Tijuana, Mexico
Flamingo Casino, New Orleans, Louisiana
Fort Garry Hotel, Winnepeg, Manitoba, Canada
Fortinum's Fountain, London, England
Forum of the Twelve Sisters, New York City, New York
Fouquet's Restaurant, Paris, France
Four Ways, Washington, DC
Franco's Italian Restaurant, Milwaukee, Wisconsin
Frank & Marie's, Chicago, Illinois
French Port, Chicago, Illinois
Frere Jacques, Chicago, Illinois
Fritzel's, Chicago, Illinois
Gage and Tollner's, New York City, New York
Galatoire's, New Orleans, Louisiana
Gale's Street Inn, Chicago, Illinois
Ganges, London, England
Garavelli Buffet, St Louis, Missouri
Gaslight Club, Chicago, Illinois
Gaslight Club, Ohare Airport, Chicago, Illinois
Gavroche Bistro, Chicago, Illinois
Gaylord India Restaurant, Hong Kong
Gaylord India Restaurant, Chicago, Illinois
Gaylord India Restaurant, London, England
Gaylord India Restaurant, New Delhi, India
Gaylord India Restaurant, Trinidad, Tobago
Gaylord India Restaurant, Bombay, India
Getranke, Dusseldorf, Germany
Gianotti, Chicago, Illinois
Giordano's, Chicago, Illinois
Glossops, Toronto, Ontario Canada
Golden Gourmet, Bangkok, Thailand
Golden Mushroom, Southfield, Michigan
Golden Ox, Chicago, Illinois
Golden Star Steak & Lobster, New Orleans, Louisiana
Good Life, Chicago, Illinois
Grand Central Station, Oyster Bar, New York City, New York
Grand Hotel, Oslo, Norway
Grand Hotel, Stockholm, Sweden
Grande Bertagne Hotel, Athens, Greece
Grandstand Grill, Kowloon, Hong Kong
Graycliff, Nassau, Bahamas
Great Pizza Pie Experience, Chicago, Illinois
Grill & Cue, Boston, Massachusetts
Grisanti's, Memphis, Tennessee

Gritti Palace, Venice, Italy
Grosvenor House, Park Lane, London, England
Groundhog Tavern, Atlanta, Georgia
Guey Sam, Chicago, Illinois
Half Shell, Chicago, Illinois
Forum of the Twelve Caesars ... New York City ... USA
Friar's Club ... New York City ... USA
Galatoire's ... New Orleans ... USA
Grand Station Station Oyster Bar ... New York City ... USA
Grisanti's ... Memphis ... USA
Harrah's Hotel and Casino, Lake Tahoe, Nevada
Harrod's, London, England
Harry Carey's, Chicago, Illinois
Harry's Bar, Venice, Italy
Harry's New York Bar, Paris, France
Hashikin, Chicago, Illinois
Hatsuhana, Chicago, Illinois
Haverford School, Haverford, Pennsylvania
Heaven's Restaurant, Pittsburgh, Pennsylvaia
Hennesey's, Chicago, Illinois
Henrici Restaurant & Café, Chicago, Illinois
Henry's, Key West, Florida
Hilton Hotel & Tower, San Francisco, Illinois
Hilton Hotel New Orleans, New Orleans,
Harrods ... London ... England
Harry's Bar ... Venice ... Italy
Harry's Cafe ... Chicago ... USA
Ho Shun Restaurant, New York City, New York
Hoe Choy Restaurant, Chicago, Illinois
Hole in the Wall, Bath, England
Holstein's, Chicago, Illinois
Hong Kong Bay, Chicago, Illinois
Horcher, Madrid, Spain
Hostellerie de la Poste, Avallon, France
Hostellerie de Vieux Cordes, Cordes, France
Hole in the Wall ... Bath ... England
Hostellerie de la Poste ... Avallon ... France
Hotel Danieli, Venice, Italy
Hotel de la Poste, Beaune, France
Hotel du Lac, Geneva, Switzerland
Hotel du Palais, Biarritz, France
Hotel Excelsior, Naples, Italy
Hotel George V, Paris, France
Hotel Hana-Maui, Honolulu, Hawaii
Hotel Inter-Continental Kinshasa, Zaire, Africa
Hotel Inter-Continental, Hilton Head, South Carolina
Hotel Inter-Continental, New York City, New York
Hotel Inter-Continental, Zagreb, Yugoslavia
Hotel Le Prince de Galles, Paris, France
Hotel Le Warwick, Paris, France
Hotel Malibu Beach Bar, Acapulco, Mexico
Hotel Melia Granada, Granada

Hotel Muehlebach, Kansas City, Kansas
Hotel Pulitzer, Amsterdam, Holland
Hotel St. Regis, New York City, New York
Hotel Viking. Oslo, Norway
Hotellerie du Bas Breau, Paris, France
Hotellerie du Bas, Barbizon, France
Houlihan's, New Orleans, Louisiana
House of Chan, New York City, New York
House of Dong Yuant, Chicago, Illinois
House of Hunan, Chicago, Illinois
House of India, Chicago, Illinois
House of Prime Rib, San Francisco, California
House of Ribs, Chicago, Illinois
Hunan Chinese Restaurant, Carbondale, Illinois
Hunan Star, Skokie, Illinois
Hunan Taste, New York City, New York
Hunan Village, Murphysboro, Illinois
Hunt Room Grill, New Orleans, Louisiana
Hyatt Regency Water Tower, Chicago, Illinois
Hyatt Regency, Atlanta, Georgia
Il Club del Doge, Venice, Italy
Illinois Central Main Line of America, Chicago, Illinois
Imperial Hotel, Tokyo, Japan
India House, San Francisco, California
Inigo Jones, London, England
Innsbrook, Tarpon, Florida
Ireland's Oyster House, Chicago, Illinois
Ireland's, Chicago, Illinois
J.P.'s Eating Place, Chicago, Illinois
Jack & Esther's Seafood House, Chicago, Illinois
Jack's Restaurant, San Francisco, California
Jacques French Restaurant, Chicago, Illinois
Jasand's, Chicago, Illinois
Hotel de la Poste ... Beaune ... France
Hotel Hana-Maui ... Hawaii ... USA
Irelands ... Chicago ... USA
Jasper Park Lodge, Jasper, Alberta, Canada
Jazz & Mo Jazz, New Orleans, Louisiana
Jeff's Laugh-Inn Lounge, Chicago, Illinois
Jefferson Avenue Boarding House, St Louis, Missouri
Jefferson Hotel, St. Louis, Missouri
Jefferson Hotel, Washington, D.C.
Jicarilla Apache Cocktail Lounge, Dulce, New Mexico
Jimmy Wong's, Chicago, Illinois
Jim's Pizza Place, Carbondale, Illinois
Jockey Club, Washington, DC
Jockey, Madrid, Spain
Joe Muer Sea Food, Detroit, Michigan
John Barleycorn, Chicago, Illinois, Louisiana

John Dominis, Honolulu, Hawaii
Johnny's Lounge, Chicago, Illinois
Jonathan B Club, Chicago, Illinois
Kabby's Seafood Restaurant, New Orleans, Louisiana
Kabby's Sports Edition & Grille, New Orleans, Louisiana
Kabuki of Chicago, Chicago, Illinois
Kahala Hilton Hotel, Honolulu, Hawaii
Kan's, San Francisco, California
Kaplan's, Houston, Texas
Karl Ratzsch's, Milwaukee, Wisconsin
Kazan Restaurant, Ankara, Turkey
Kelly Mondelli's, Chicago, Illinois
Kemolls Restaurant, St Louis, Missouri
Kempinski Hotel, Berlin Germany
Kenessey Gourmets Internationale, Chicago, Illinois
King Crab, Chicago, Illinois
King's View Dining Room, Rosemont, Illinois
King's Wharf, Lincolnshire, Illinois
Kon Tike Bar and Restaurant, Albequerque, New Mexico
Kon Tiki Ports, Chicago, Illinois
K-Paul's Louisiana Kitchen, New Orleans, Louisiana
Kronehalle, Zurich, Switzerland
Kuala Lumpur Hilton, Kuala Lumpur, Malaysia
Kuo Wah Restaurant, San Francisco, California
La Belle Sole, Oslo, Norway
La Boule d'Or, Paris, France
La Calvados Apple Brandy Bar Restaurant, Paris, France
La Caravelle, New York City, New York
La Costa Hotel and Spa, Carlsbad, California
La Cremaillere, Banksville, New York
La Gauloise, New Orleans, Louisiana
La Mallorquina, Old San Juan, Puerto Rico
La Mediterranee, Paris, France
La Mer, Chicago, Illinois
La Plaza, Key West, Florida
La Reserve, Beaulieu-sur-Mer, France
La Terraza, Chicago, Illinois
La Terraza, Evanston, Illinois
La Tour D'Argent, Paris, France
Ladles and Lobsters, Chicago, Illinois
Lafitte's Old Absinthe House, New Orleans, Louisiana
Lake Louis Lodge, Lake Louis, Banff, Canada
Lasserre, Paris, France
Le Bistro de Paris, Paris, France
Le Diner, Hamilton, Bermuda
Le Festival, Chicago, Illinois
Le Francais, Wheeling, Illinois
Le Madrilene, New York City, New York
Le Nomad, Chicago, Illinois
Le Pavillon de L'Atlantique, Montreal, Quebec Canada
Le Pavillon de L'Atlantique, Ottawa, Ontario Canada

Le Pavillon Elysee, Paris, France
Le Pavillon, New York City, New York
Le Perroquet, Chicago, Illinois
Le Pub, Chicago Illinois
Le Vauban, Paris, France
Jockey Club ... Madrid ... Spain
La Belle Sole ... Oslo ... Norway
La Boule d'Or ... Paris ... France
La Cremailler ... Banksville ... USA
La Madrilene, New York City, New York
La Madrilene ... New York City ... USA
La Mallorquina ... Puerto Rico ... USA
La Perroquet ... Chicago ... USA
La Reserve ... Beaulieu-sur-Mer ... Marseilles Coast ... France
Ladles and Lobsters ... Chicago ... USA
Lamb's Club ... New York City ... USA
Le Pavillon ... New York City ... USA
Gage and Tollner's ... Brooklyn ... USA
Lee's Cantan Café, Chicago, Illinois
Legal Sea Foods, Boston, Massachusetts
Leona's, Chicago, Illinois
Les Copaines, Toronto, Ontario Canada
Les Violins, Miami, Florida
L'Escargot on Halsted, Chicago, Illinois
L'Espalier, Boston, Massachusetts
Levens Hall, Westmoreland, England
L'Hotel de L'Aigle Noir, Fontainebleu, France
Lisi's Hors d"Oeuvres, Chicago, Illinois
Little Venice, New York City, New York
Lobster Pound, Chicago, Illinois
Locke-Ober's. Boston, Massachusetts
Loew's Anatole Hotel, Dallas Texas
London's Savoy Hotel, London, England
L'Orangerie, San Francisco, California
Lord Chumley's, St Charles, Illinois
Louie's Backyard, Key West, Florida
Louis XVI Restaurant, New Orleans, Louisiana
Luchow's, New York City, New York
Luigi's, New York City, New York
Luigi's, St Louis, Missouri
Lutece, New York City, New York
MacDonald Hotel, Edmonton, Alberta, Canada
Maharaja Restaurant, Chicago, Illinois
Mai Kai Polynesian Restaurant, Ft. Lauderdale, Florida
Mandarin House, Chicago, Illinois
Mandarin House, San Francisco, California
Mandar-Inn, Chicago, Illinois
Mangia Italiano, Chicago, Illinois
Map Room, Chicago, Illinois

Maple Leaf Bar, New Orleans, Louisiana
Marie Cristina Hotel, San Sebastian, Spain
Mariott Marquis Hotel, New York City, New York
Marius et Janette, Paris, France
Mark Hopkins Hotel, San Francisco, California
Mark II, Chicago, Illinois
Market Street Grill, Salt Lake City, UT
Mark's Chop Suey, Chicago, Illinois
Marquette Inn, Chicago, Illinois
Marriott Casa Marina, Key West, Florida
Marriott Guest Room Dining, Boston, Massachusetts
Marriott's Sam Lord's Castle, Barbados
Martingayle's Restaurant, Chicago, Illinois
Maspero's Slave Exchange, New Orleans, Louisiana
Matsuya, Chicago, Illinois
Maui Inter-Continental Wailea, Kihei, Maui, Hawaii
Mayfair Regent Hotel, New York City, New York
MGM Hotel and Casino, Las Vegas, Nevada
Mi Casa Su Casa Restaurant, Chicago, Illinois
Michael Jordan's, Chicago, Illinois
L'Espionage Club ... Washington, D.C.... USA
Levens Hall ... Westmorland..England
Liar's Club ... New York City ... USA
Locke-Ober's ... Boston ... USA
Luchow's ... New York City ... USA
Mama Leone's ... New York City ... USA
Michaul's on St. Charles, New Orleans, Louisiana
Mickey Finn's, Seattle, Washington
Mike Serio's Po-Boys and Deli, New Orleans, Louisiana
Miller's Steak House, Chicago, Illinois
Mingei-Ya, San Francisco, California
Monique's Café, Chicago, Illinois
Monk's Inn, New York City, New York
Moonlite Bar-B-Q Inn, Owensboro, Kentucky
Mortimer Snerd's, Chicago, Illinois
Mother Hubbard's, Chicago, Illinois
Mountain Jacks, Farmington Hills, Michigan
Mr Chop Suey #3, Chicago, Illinois
Mr. B's Bistro, New Orleans, Louisiana
Mt. Kenya Safari Club, Nanyuki, Kenya
Myro and Phil's, Chicago, Illinois
Napoleon House, New Orleans, Louisiana
New Nan Yen Resteurent, Chicago, Illinois
New Orleans Apothecary, New Orleans, Louisiana
New York Hilton, New York City, New York

Mortimer Snerd's ... Chicago ... USA
Newport Yacht Club, Newport, Rhode Island
Nola, New Orleans, Louisiana
Noodles, Toronto, Ontario Canada
Normandy Hotel, Paris, France
Oak Room Bar, Hotel Plaza, New York City, New York
Oceana, Boston, Massachusetts
O'Fame, Chicago, Illinois
Old Angus, Washington, DC
Old Carolina Crab House, Chicago, Illinois
Old Farm House, Chicago, Illinois
Old Jerusalem, Chicago, Illinois
Old Original Bookbinder's, Philadelphia, Pennsylvania
Olive Oil's. Lake Geneva, Wisconsin
Omni Hotel, Miami Springs, Florida
Once Upon a Thai, Chicago, Illinois
Oodles of Noodles, Chicago, Illinois
Opryland Hotel, Nashville, Tennessee
Original French Market, New Orleans, Louisiana
Overton's, London, England
Oxford's Pub, Chicago, Illinois
Oyster Bar, Waldorf-Astoria, New York City, New York
P. O. E. T. S., Chicago, Illinois
Pagoda Inn, Chicago, Illinois
Palace Hotel, Brussels, Belgium
Palace Hotel, Madrid, Spain
Palace Hotel, San Francisco, California
Pali Kai, Evanston, Illinois
Palm Court, Plaza Hotel, New York City, New York
Palmer House, Chicago, Illinois
Pam Pam West, Kansas City, Missouri
Panorama Room, Portland, Oregon
Papa Milano, Chicago, Illinois
Papa's III, Chicago, Illinois
Paradise Café, Chicago, Illinois
Park Lane Hotel, New York City, New York
Parker House, Boston, Massachusetts
Parthenon Restaurant, Chicago, Illinois
Old Original Bookbinder's ... Philadelphia ... USA
Oodles of Noodles ... Chicago ... USA
Lasserre ... Paris ... France
Palace Hotel ... Madrid ... Spain
Papa Lobster ... Chicago ... USA
Pascal's Manale Restaurant, New Orleans, Louisiana
Passetto, Rome, Italy
Patout's Cajun Corner, New Orleans, Louisiana
Patout's Restaurant, New Orleans, Louisiana
Paul Bunyan's Blue Ox Bar, Mt. Hood, Oregon
Pearl Restaurant & Oyster Bar, New Orleans, Louisiana
Pentola Pizzeria, Chicago, Illinois
Perino's, Los Angeles, California
Peter Lo's Mandarin Restaurant, Chicago, Illinois

Peter's Backyard, Greenwich Village, New York
Pete's, Boca Raton, Florida
Petra Forum Hotel, Petra, Jordan
Pheasant Run, St Charles, Illinois
Philly's, Chicago, Illinois
Piccadilly Hotel, London, England
Pier House, Key West, Florida
Pierre Grill, New York City, New York
Pippin's Tavern, Chicago, Illinois
Place Vendome, Paris, France
Playboy Club, Chicago, Illinois
Playboy Club, Lake Geneva, Wisconsin
Playboy Club, London, England
Playboy Club, Los Angeles, California
Playboy Club, New Orleans, Louisiana
Playboy Club, New York City, New York
Playboy Club, San Francisco, California
Playboy Club, St. Louis, Missouri
Playboy Club, Tokyo, Japan
Plunkett Catering, Chicago, Illinois
Pontchartrain Hotel, New Orleans, Louisiana
Popeye's Galley & Grog, Lake Geneva, Wisconsin
Pops for Champagne, Chicago, Illinois
Portales, Merida, Mexico
Passetto ... Rome ... Italy
Perino's ... Los Angeles ... USA
Pierre Grille ... New York City ... USA
Prince of Wales, Chicago, Illinois
Pronto, Chicago, Illinois
Pump Room, Ambassador's East, Chicago, Illinois
Pyramid, Appleton, Wisconsin
Ramponneau, Paris, France
Ranalli's Off Rush, Chicago, Illinois
Ranalli's, Chicago, Illinois
Rathskeller, Toronto, Ontario Canada
Ratskeller Munchen, Munich, Germany
Red Barn, Madison, Wisconsin
Red Star Inn, Chicago, Illinios
Red Star Inn, Chicago, Illinois
Registry Resort, Scottsdale, Arizona
Remington on Post Oak Park, Houston, Texas
Renaldi's Pizza, Chicago, Illinois
Restaurant Blom, Oslo, Norway
Restaurant Horcher, Madrid, Spain
Restaurant Named Desire, Chicago, Illinois
Restaurant Sazerac, New Orleans, Louisiana
Restaurantes Los Almendros, Yucatan, Mexico
Rib Room-Royal Orleans, New Orleans, Louisiana
Richmond Hotel, Copenhagen, Denmark
Ristorante Cittadella, Rome, Italy
Ristorante Pierluigi, Rome, Italy
Ristorante Saraceno, Boston, Massachusetts
Ritz Hotel, Madrid, Spain
Ritz-Carlton, Atlanta, Georgia
Rivoli, Mexico City, Mexico

Robbie's, Decatur, Illinois
Robbie's, Springfield, Illinois
Roditas, Chicago, Illinois
Rooney's, Chicago, Illinois
Roosevelt Grill, New York City, New York
Roosevelt Hotel, New Orleans, Louisiana
Rosario's, Chicago, Illinois
Royal Caribbean Hotel, Kingston, Jamaican
Royal Caribbean Hotel, Montego Bay, Jamaican
Royal Orleans, New Orleans, Louisiana
Royal Sonesta Hotel, New Orleans, Louisiana
Royal York Hotel, Toronto, Ontario, Canada
Ruby Foo's, Montreal, Quebec Canada
Russian Tea Room, New York City, New York
Rusty Pelican, San Francisco, California
Ryan House, Dubuque, Iowa
S. S. Bremen, North German Lloyd Line
S. S. Normandie, The French Line, Marseilles, France
S.S. New York, Hamburg-American Line, New York
Sabrina de Botin, Madrid, Spain
Sage's East, Chicago, Illinois
Sage's Sinner's Club, Chicago, Illinois
Sally's Key West, Chicago, Illinois
Sally's Key West, Key West, Florida

Salvador's, Chicago, Illinois
Sam-Mee Restaurant, Chicago, Illinois
Samurai, Chicago, Illinois
San Marcos Room, San Francisco, Illinois
Sanborn's, Monterey, California
Sanborn's, San Francisco, California
Sanborn's, Acapulco, Mexico
Sanborn's, Del Angel, Spain
Sanborn's, Del Prado, Spain
Sanborn's, Insurgentes, Spain
Sanborn's, Universidad, Spain
Sandpiper and Tradewinds, St. Petersburg, Florida
Sanko, Chicago, Illinois
Sardi's, New York City, New York
Scandia, Los Angeles, California
Schuylkill Club, Philadelphia, Pennsylvania
Scoglio di Frisio, Rome, Italy
Scratch Restaurant, Santa Minica, California
Sea Pines Plantation, Hilton Head, South Carolina
Seafood Circus, Chicago, Illinois
Seaport Cajun Café & Bar, New Orleans,
Restaurant Blom ... Oslo ... Norway
Restaurant de la Pyramide de la Point ... Vienne ... France
Restaurant Horcher ... Madrid ... Spain
Ritz Hotel ... Madrid ... Spain
Rivoli ... Mecico City ... Mexico
Sabrina de Botin ... Madrid ... USA
Sardi's ... New York City ... USA
Scandia ... Los Angeles ... USA

Second City, Chicago, Illinois
Select Cut, Chicago, Illinois
Semiramis Hotel, Cairo, Egypt
Senor Pico, Los Angeles, California
Senor Pico, San Francisco, California
Seven Seas Bar and Grill, San Diego, California
Shanghai Inn, St Louis, Missouri
Shanghaii, Chicago, Illinois
Sheapard's Hotel, Cairo, Egypt
Shepheard's Hotel, Cairo, Egypt
Sheraton Hong Kong Hotel, Kowloon, Hong Kong
Sheraton Houston Hotel, Houston, Texas
Sheraton-Cadillac Hotel, Detroit, Michigan
Shezan, London, England
Shirreffs, London, England
Amstel Hotel ... Amsterdam ... Holland
Shogun, Houston, Texas
Shore Club, Lake Geneva, Wisconsin
Shucker's, Chicago, Illinois
Siam Corner, Chicago, Illinois
Single File, Chicago, Illinois
Skylon, Niagara Falls, Ontario Canada
Smuggler's Cove, Wheeling, Illinois
Snuggery Saloon, Chicago, Illinois
Soley, Barcelona, Spain
Somebody Else's Troubles, Chicago, Illinois
Sonesta Beach Hotel, Key Biscayne, Florida
Star of Thailand, Chicago, Illinois
Star Steak & Lobster House, New Orleans, Louisiana
Starlight Roof, New York City, New York
Statler Hotel, New York City, New York
Steak & Lobster Restaurant, Chicago, Illinois
Stefani's, Chicago, Illinois
Stephenson's Apple Farm, Kansas City, Missouri
Sterch's, Chicago, Illinois
Stonehenge, Ridgefield, New York
Streeter's Tavern, Chicago, Illinois
Su Casa, Chicago, Illinois
Sun Luck, New York City, New York
Szechwan & Hunan Fine Cusine, Chicago, Illinois
Szechwan House, Chicago, Illinois
Sanborn's, Lindavista, Spain
Sanborn's, Madero, Spain
Sanborn's, Manacar, Spain
Sanborn's, Niza, Spain
Sanborn's, Palacio, Spain
Sanborn's, Pueblo, Puerto Rica
Sanborn's, Reforma, Spain
Sanborn's, San Angel, Spain
Taj Majal Hotel, Bombay, India
Tamdris, Munich, Germany
Tango Diner, Chicago, Illinois
Tap Root Pub Beer Garden, Chicago, Illinois
Taverna Ta Nissia Story, Athens, Greece
Texas Star Fajita Bar, Chicago, Illinois
Thai Touch, Chicago, Illinois

The Absinthe Bar, New Orleans, Louisiana
The Black Knight, Lake Geneva, Wisconsin
Sobrino de Botin ... Madrid ... Spain
Soley ... Barcelona ... Spain
Stonehenge ... Ridgefield ... USA
The Bakery ... Chicago ... USA
The Bali ... Amsterdam ... Holland
The Blue Fox, San Francisco, California
The Brass Rail, Pleasantville, New York
The Cartoon Club, Chicago, Illinois
The Circus, Chicago, Illinois
The Blue Fox ... San Francisco ... USA
The Cock n' Bull Lounge, Washington, D.C.
The Crouching Lion, Kahuku, Oahu, Hawaii
The Drake Hotel, Chicago, Illinois
The Dunes Club, Naragansett, Rhode Island
The Earl of Old Town, Chicago, Illinois
The Four Seasons, New York City, New York
The Dunes Club ... Narragansett Beach ... USA
The Four Seasons ... New York City ... USA
The Gallery Restaurant, Lake Forest, Illinois
The Gargoyle, Lake Geneva, Wisconsin
The Grand Hyatt Hotel, New York City, New York
The Gresham Hotel, Dublin, Ireland
The Hange-Uppe, Chicago, Illinois
The Hubba Hubba Club, Honolulu, Hawaii
The Ivy, London, England
The Lodge at Pebble Beach, Pebble Beach, California
The Lodge, Chicago, Illinois
The Mansion on Turtle Creek, Dallas, Texas
The Merryland Club, San Diego, California
The Mushroom, Stoughton, Wisconsin
The Office, Albuquerque, New Mexico
The Old Carolina Crab House, Chicago, Illinois
The Oyster, Chicago, Illinois
The Palmer House, Chicago, Illinois
The Pinehurst, Pinehurst, North Carolina
The Racquet Club, Palm Springs, California
The Rainforest, Chicago, Illinois
The Ivy ... London ... England
The Jockey Club ... New York City ... USA
The Moulin Rouge ... Paris ... France
The Pump Room ... Chicago ... USA
The Racquet Club ... Palm Springs ... USA

The Ranch Supper Club, Swisher, Iowa
The Red Carpet, Chicago, Illinois
The Red Star Line, London, England
The Ritz Hotel, Paris France
The Red Carpet ... Chicago ... USA
The Ritz-Carlton, Chicaago, Illinois
The Royal Danieli Roof Terrace,
The Royal Danieli Roof Terrace ... Venice ... Italy
The Royal New Orleans ... New Orleans ... USA
The Santa Fe Super Chief ... USA
The Seafood Circus ... Chicago ... USA
The Stockyard Inn ... Chicago ... USA
The Warwick ... Philadelphia ... USA
The Whitehall Club ... Chicago ... USA
Tour d'Argent ... Paris ... France
Trader Vic's ... Chicago ... USA
Trader Vic's ... New York City ... USA
Tre Scalini ... Rome ... Italy
Virginia Museum of Fine Arts ... Richmond ... USA
Waldorf Astoria, New York City, New York
Walnut Inn, Carbondale, Illinois
Walrus & The Carpenter, Toronto, Ontario Canada
Warwick Hotel, Philadelphia, Pennsylvania
Waterfront, The, Chicago, Illinois
Waves Bar & Grill, Boston, Massachusetts
Wayside Inn, South Sudbury, New York
Whiskey's Smokehouse, Boston, Massachusetts
Whistle Stop, Kalamazoo, Michigan
Windows of the World, New York City, New York
Windsor Arms Hotel, Toronto, Ontario Canada
Winstead's Steakburgers, Kansas City, Missouri
Wittles, Toronto, Ontario, Canada
Woburn Abbey, Buckinghamshire, England
Woks, Chicago, Illinois
Wrigley's Men's Bar, Chicago, Illinois
Wyndham Hotel, Dallas, Texas
Ye Cottage Inn, Keyport, New Jersey
Ye Olde Union Oyster House, Boston, Massachusetts
Yes Sir, Senator, Chicago, Illinois
Zum Bocfchen, Frankfort, Germany
Zur Alten Munce, Munich, Germany
Wayside Inn ... South Sudbury ... USA
Woburn Alley ... Buckinghamshire ... England
Wrigley Building Men's Bar ... Chicago ... USA

Index

Abalone with Olive Oil and Butter 128
Aioli Sauce 152
Angels on Horseback 15

Basic Pie Crust 23, 24, 178
Basted Seafood Skewers 105
Bay Scallops in Button Mushrooms 24
B-B-Q Sauce 158
Béarnaise Sauce 153
Béchamel Sauce 10, 11, 42, 119, 127, 128, 151, 152, 154, 156
Beef Stock I 119, 120, 162
Beef Stock II 162
Beer and Oyster Soup 46
Beer Shrimp 2
Billi-Bi Soup 52
Black Roux 176
Blackened Cajun Fish 91
Blonde Roux 176
Blue Crab Soup with Picada 53
Bouquet Garni I 92, 120, 138, 155, 162, 164, 165, 168, 172
Bouquet Garni II 120, 138, 164, 165, 168, 172
Bouquet Garni IV 162, 172
Bouquet Garni V 173
Bouquet Garni VI 173
Brown Roux 176
Buckingham Eggs 26

Cardinal Sauce 133, 134, 135, 136, 151
Caviar 4, 5, 6, 11, 12, 25, 26, 27, 67, 71, 103, 104

Caviar Supreme 5
Chicken Stock 7, 8, 28, 43, 45, 52, 53, 94, 95, 115, 122, 131, 146, 155, 163
Chipotle Butter 89, 170
Clam Broth 18, 47, 48, 50, 58, 119
Clam Stock 165
Clams Normande 17
Clams with Mop sauce 141
Clarified Butter 24, 154, 168
Coconut Cream 106, 107, 115, 174
Codfish with Chipotle Butter and Black Beans in Papillote 89
Coquille St. Jacques 21
Court Bouillon 57, 83, 97, 98, 133, 134, 167, 168
Crab Boil 132, 133, 145, 176
Crab Boil Mixture 132, 133, 145, 176
Crab Cocktail 17, 54
Crab Legs Saute 145
Crab Quiche 23, 83
Crab Rice 146
Crayfish and Beer Rice 132
Cream of Crab and Avocado Soup 44
Cream Sauce I 21, 156, 157, 180
Cream Sauce II 156, 157
Cream Sauce IV 157
Cream Sauce V 157
Crème Fraîche 103, 104, 174
Créole Sauce 125, 126, 151
Czarina's Eggs 25

Duxelles 100, 101, 173

Fines Herbes 2, 21, 98, 140, 171
Fish Fillets with Shrimp Sauce 105
Fish Stock 49, 50, 53, 54, 55, 56, 57, 58, 60, 83, 86, 87, 90, 91, 93, 94, 99, 100, 101, 102, 103, 104, 116, 118, 120, 123, 125, 126, 132, 133, 135, 136, 149, 151, 153, 156, 165
Florida Keys Conch Chowder 49
Fruits of the Sea 21

Gefilte Fish 30, 31, 59
Glace de Viande 123, 174
Glazed Carrots 96, 182
Golden Roux 91, 101, 102, 118, 132, 176
Green Butter 169, 170
Green Mayonnaise 35, 177
Gregoire Sauce 153

Halibut with Wild Mushrooms 94
Herbal Omelet 22
Hollandaise Sauce 14, 25, 85, 154
Horseradish Sauce I 161
Horseradish Sauce II 161
Hot Like Hell Horseradish 127, 179
Hot Like Hell Mustard 11, 34, 127, 180
Hushpuppies ix, 36, 37

Jellied Seafood Consomme 58

Lobster Bisque 54, 55, 119
Lobster Cocktail 17
Lobster Minestrone 45
Lobster Quiche 23
Lobster Stock 45, 46, 112, 113, 119, 166
Lobster Tails with Black Beans 117

Maine Lobster with Majestic Cocktail Sauce 112
Maine Lobster with Parsley Butter 114

Maitre D'Hotel Butter 168
Majestic Cocktail Sauce 17, 21, 36, 37, 112, 113, 159
Manhattan Clam Chowder 47, 48
Maryland Crab Bisque 56
Meat Sauce 2, 159
Mixed Seafood Bag 137
Mop Sauce 140, 141, 142, 161
Mornay Sauce 122, 152
Moules Normande 16, 17
Mussels in Herbs 21
Mussels in Tomato Sauce 139
Mussels with Fines Herbes 140
Mussels with Leeks, Saffron and Cream 139

New England Clam Chowder 48

Otak-Otak 106
Oyster Panache 14
Oyster Quiche 23
Oysters 9, 10, 11, 12, 13, 14, 15, 16, 21, 32, 34, 46, 51, 52, 64, 69, 72, 73, 75, 76, 82, 83, 104, 105, 115, 116
Oysters Bienville 10
Oysters in Champagne 14
Oysters Lucullus 11, 14
Oysters Normande 16
Oysters Rockefeller 12, 14

Paella Valenciana 69
Parsley Butter 114, 170
Parsley Potatoes 99, 181
Picada 53, 54, 173
Pistachio Crust 91, 182

Rainbow Trout Stuffing 90, 179
Raw Oyster Soup 51
Red Mayonnaise 98, 177
Red Snapper Chowder 49

Roux 91, 93, 101, 102, 118, 130, 132, 139, 155, 175, 176
Russian Eggs 27

Saffron Rice 117, 136, 138, 180
Salmon Chowder 50
Salmon Eggs Columbia River 6
Salmon in Strawberry Pepper Wine Sauce 86
Salmon Soufflé 88
Salmon Terrine 35
Salmon with Cucumber and Tomato Sauce 86
Salmon with Saffron Cream Cheese 89
Salmon with Tequila and Tomato Vinaigrette 90
Salsa Rosa 26, 122, 142, 177
Salsa Verde 32, 176
Sauce Pistou 98, 157
Scallop Bisque 56
Scallop Quiche 24
Scallop Soup 52
Scallops and Grapes 137
Scallops Flamed with Cognac 135
Scallops in Button Mushrooms 24
Scallops in Cardinal Sauce 135
Scallops with Glazed Garlic and Champagne Sauce 134
Scampi Supreme 130
Scramblers 25
Sea Bass with Mushroom Stuffing 100
Seafood Seasoning Salt 2, 21, 170
Shrimp and Artichokes in Peppery Butter Sauce 4
Shrimp Bayou 126
Shrimp Bisque 55
Shrimp Cocktail 17
Shrimp Créole 124
Shrimp Quiche 23
Shrimp Sautéed in Garlic 2
Shrimp Stock 58, 124, 125, 126, 166
Shrimp Toast 3

Shrimp Victoria 126
Smoked Mussel Soup 42
Smoked Trout Paté 6
Snails alla Romana 29
Sole Duglere 102
Sole Marguery 101
Sole Normande 104, 105
Sole Normande Riche 105
Sole with Cucumbers and Caviar 103
Sorrel Butter Chiffonade 87, 170
Soused and Stuffed Clams 17
Soused Mackerel xi, 28
Squid and Greens 143
Steamed Clams 19, 48, 58, 166
Steamed Mussels 20
Striped Bass with Flaming Fennel and Pernod 98
Stuffed Mussels 20
Stuffed Rainbow Trout 90
Swordfish Casserole 92

Tartar Sauce 27, 143, 147, 160
Tomato Paste 47, 50, 60, 86, 87, 88, 95, 97, 98, 116, 146, 158, 160, 167, 175
Tomato Purée 43, 55, 118, 120, 160, 175
Tomato Sauce 44, 49, 50, 86, 125, 139, 148, 155
Turbot with Green Peppercorns 95
Turtle Soup 42, 43
Turtle Soup Cajun Style 43

Veal Stock I 164
Veal Stock II 164
Vegetable Stock 49, 167
Velouté Sauce 104, 105, 155

Welsh Rarebit 32, 34, 35
White Wine Court Bouillon for Fish 97, 168
White Wine Sauce I 153, 180
Wild Rice 131, 181

978-0-595-49486-0
0-595-49486-2

Printed in Great Britain
by Amazon